THIS BOOK
belongs to:

_____

Baby's Name

**Emergency Names
& Contact Information:**

_____

_____

_____

Birth Statistics

Bate of Birth   Time of Birth   Day of the Week
_____   _____   _____

Present at Birth   Place of Birth   Weight
_____   _____   _____

Head Measurement   Length   Sex
_____   _____   _____

Special Notation, (if any)
_____
_____
_____
_____

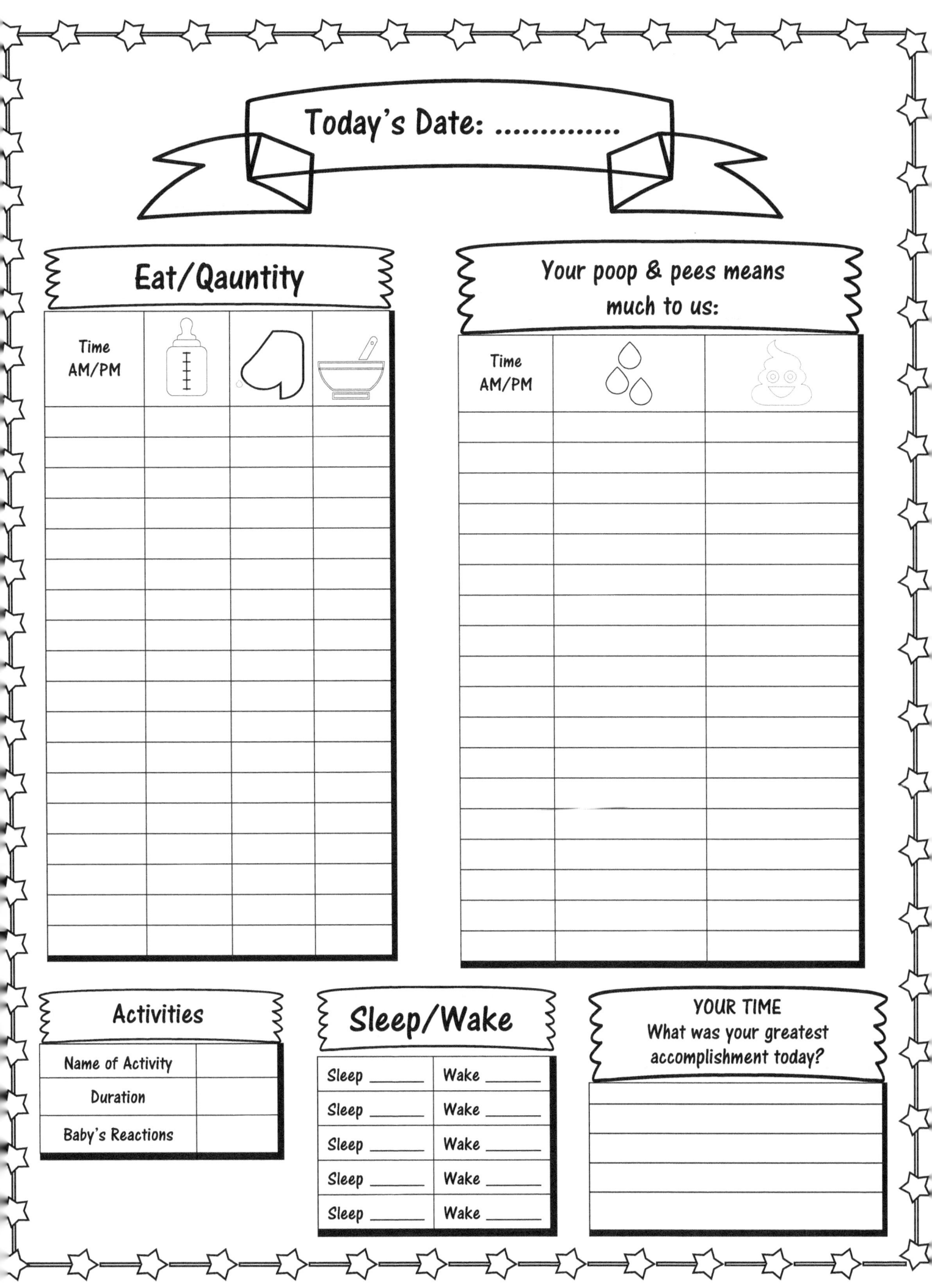

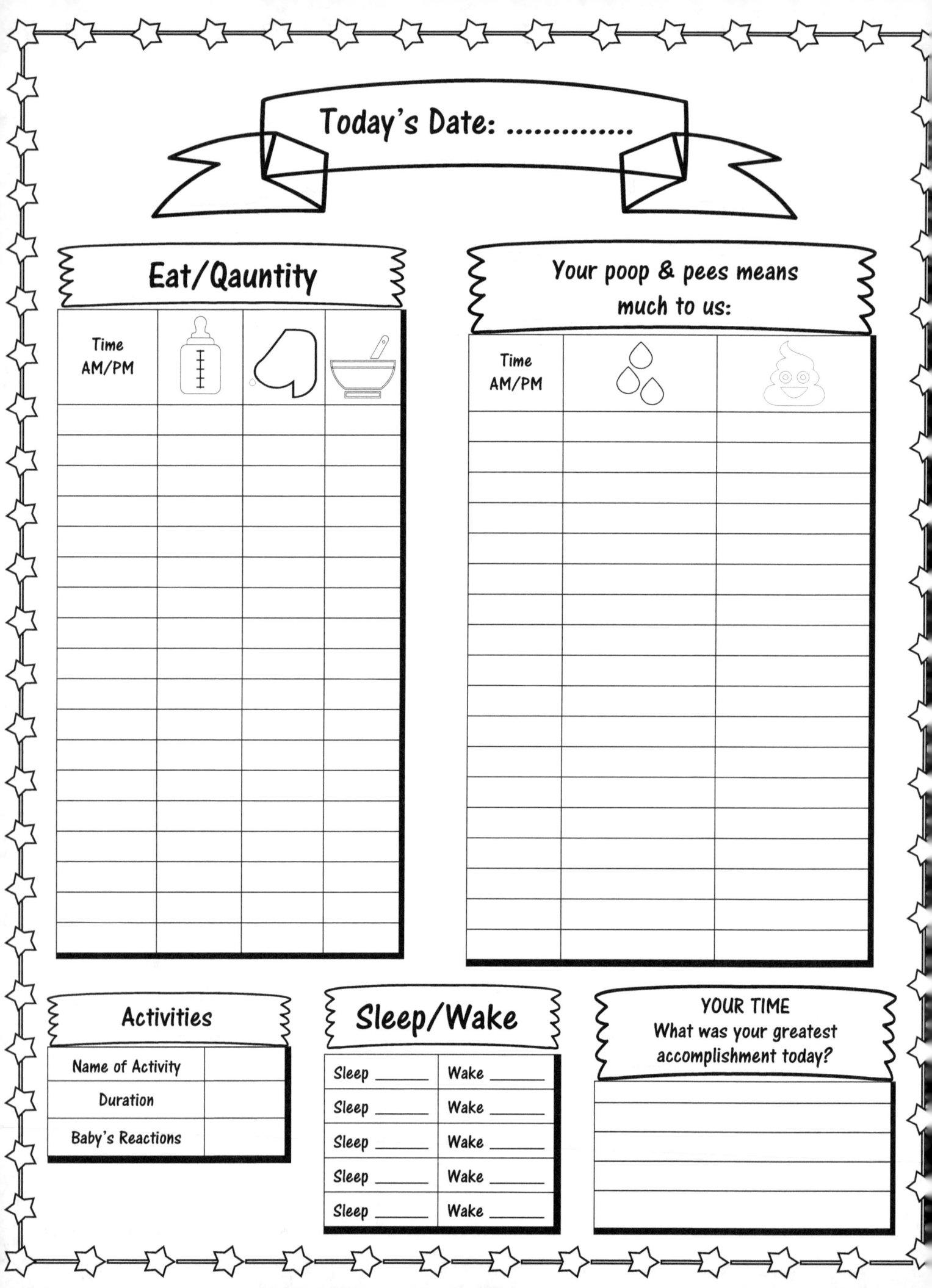

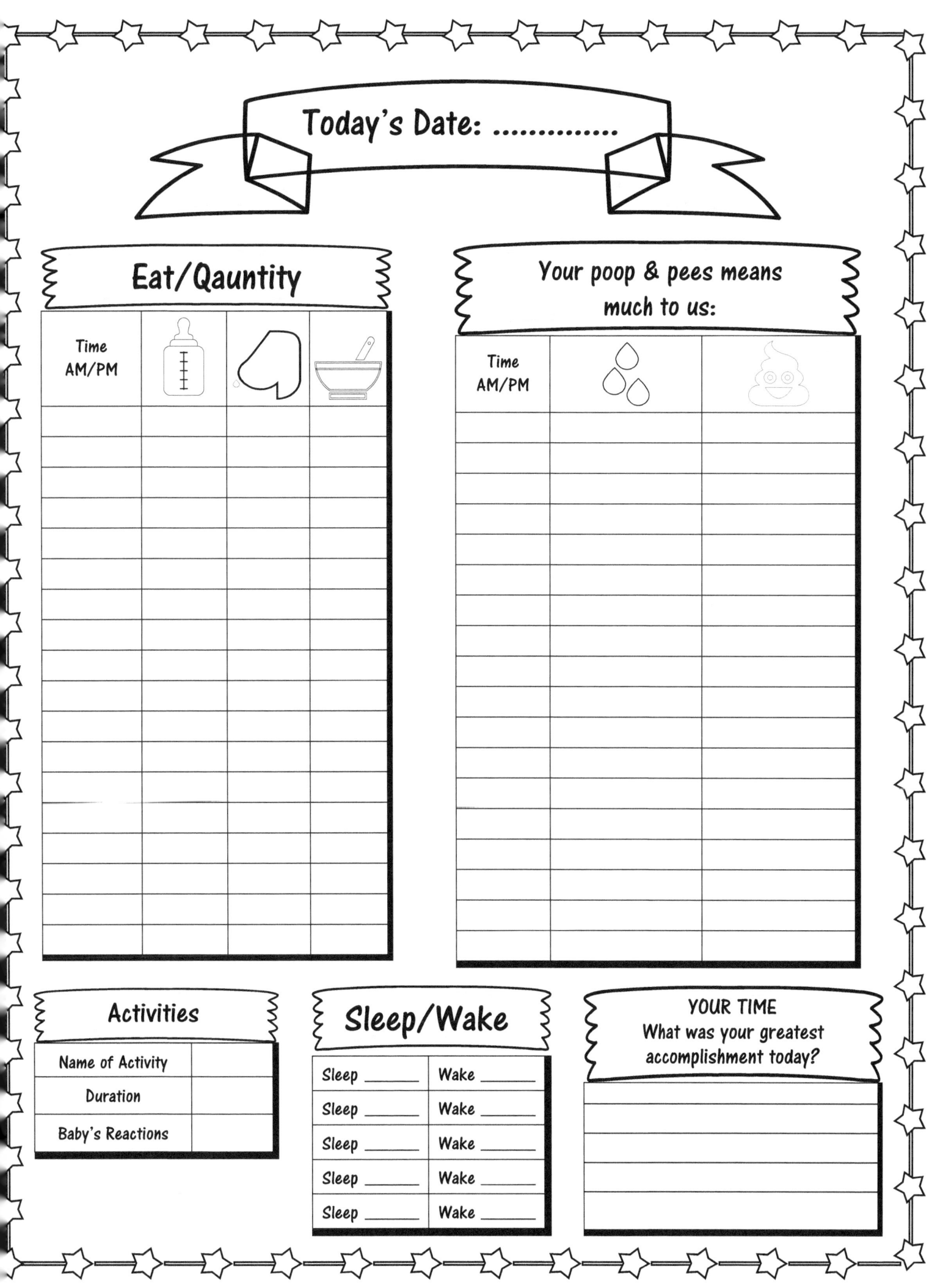

Today's Date: ....

Eat/Qauntity

Time AM/PM	🍼	💧	🥣

Your poop & pees means much to us:

Time AM/PM	💧	💩

Activities

Name of Activity	
Duration	
Baby's Reactions	

Sleep/Wake

Sleep _____ Wake _____
Sleep _____ Wake _____
Sleep _____ Wake _____
Sleep _____ Wake _____
Sleep _____ Wake _____

YOUR TIME
What was your greatest accomplishment today?

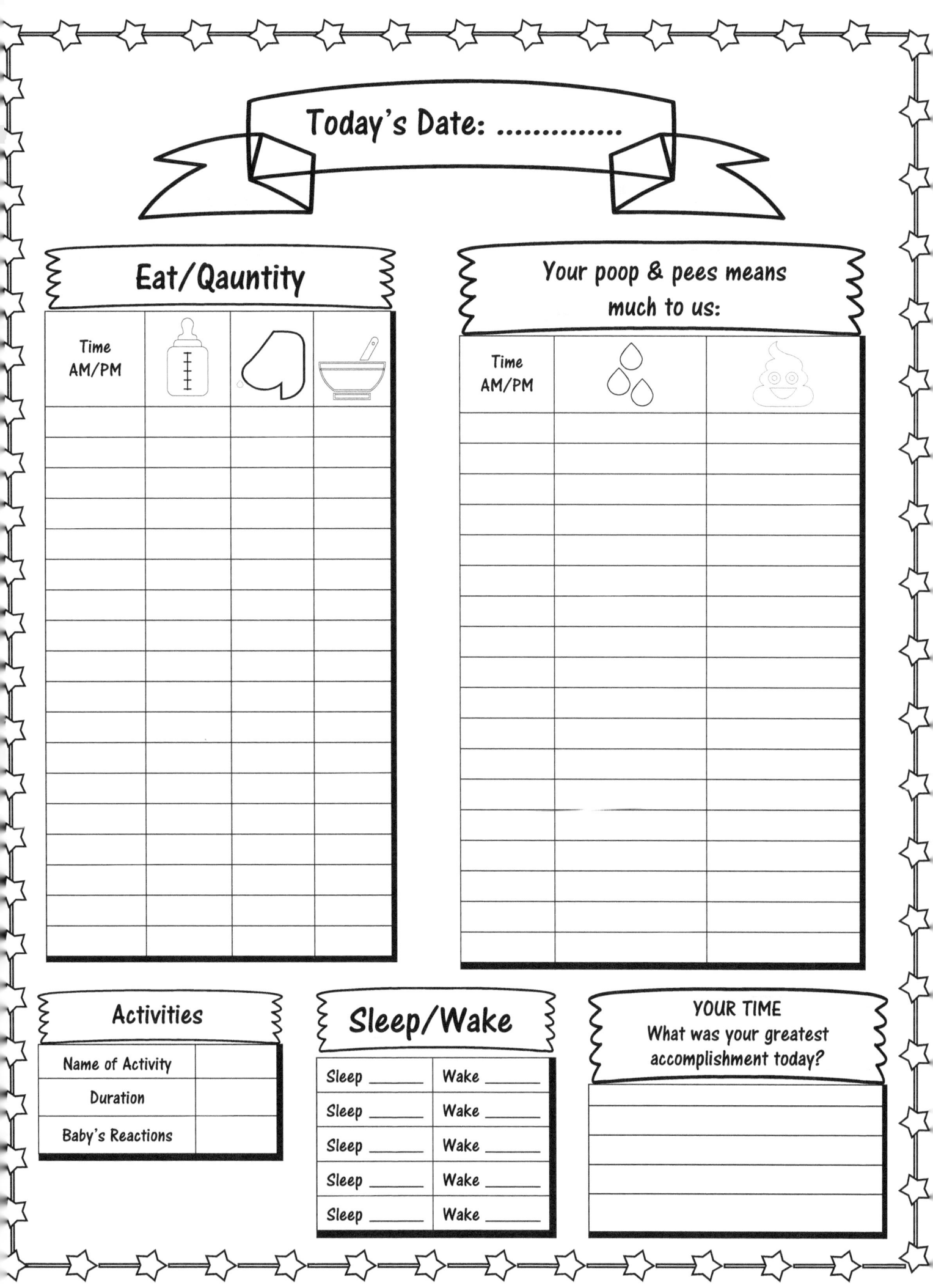

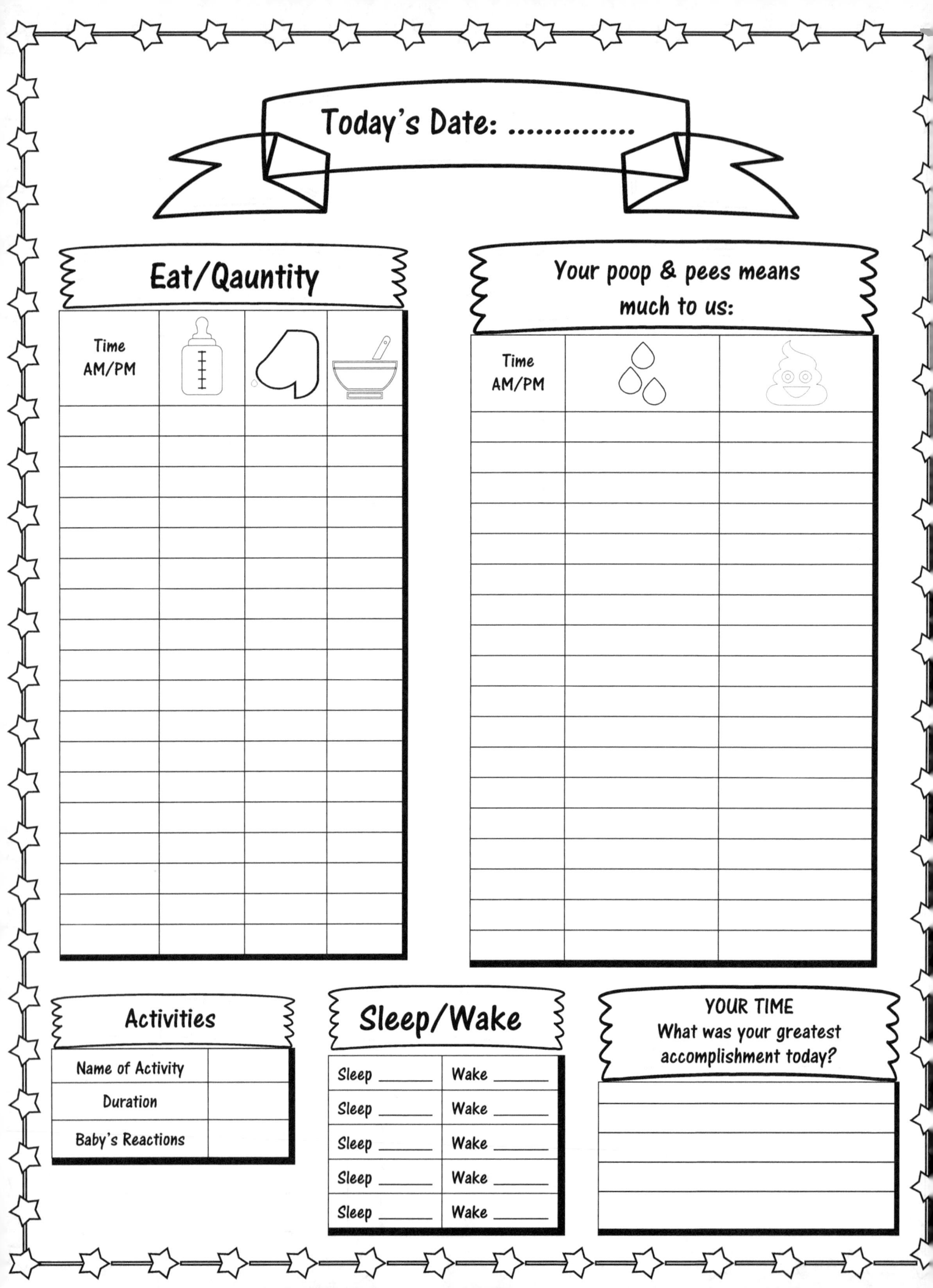

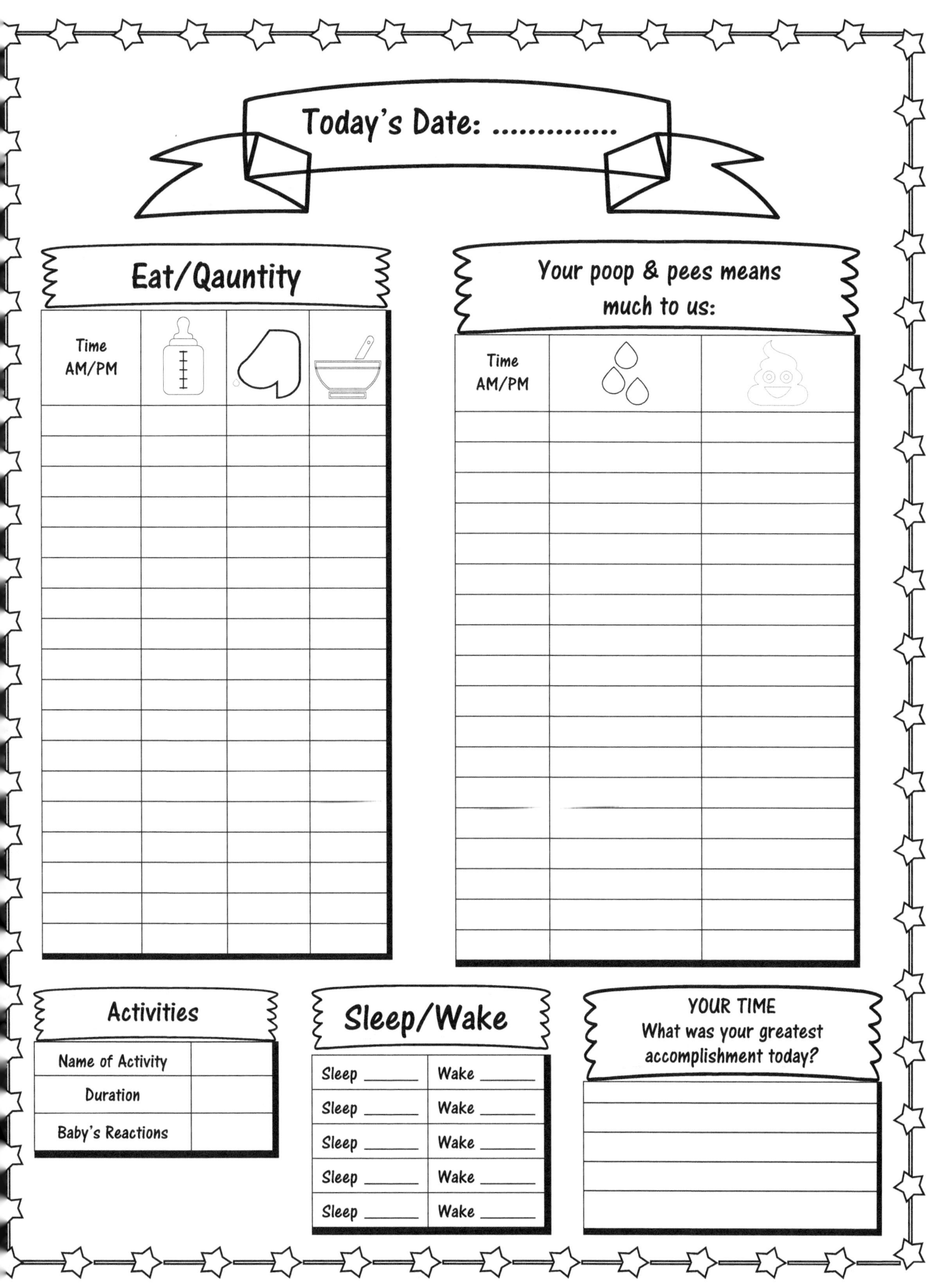

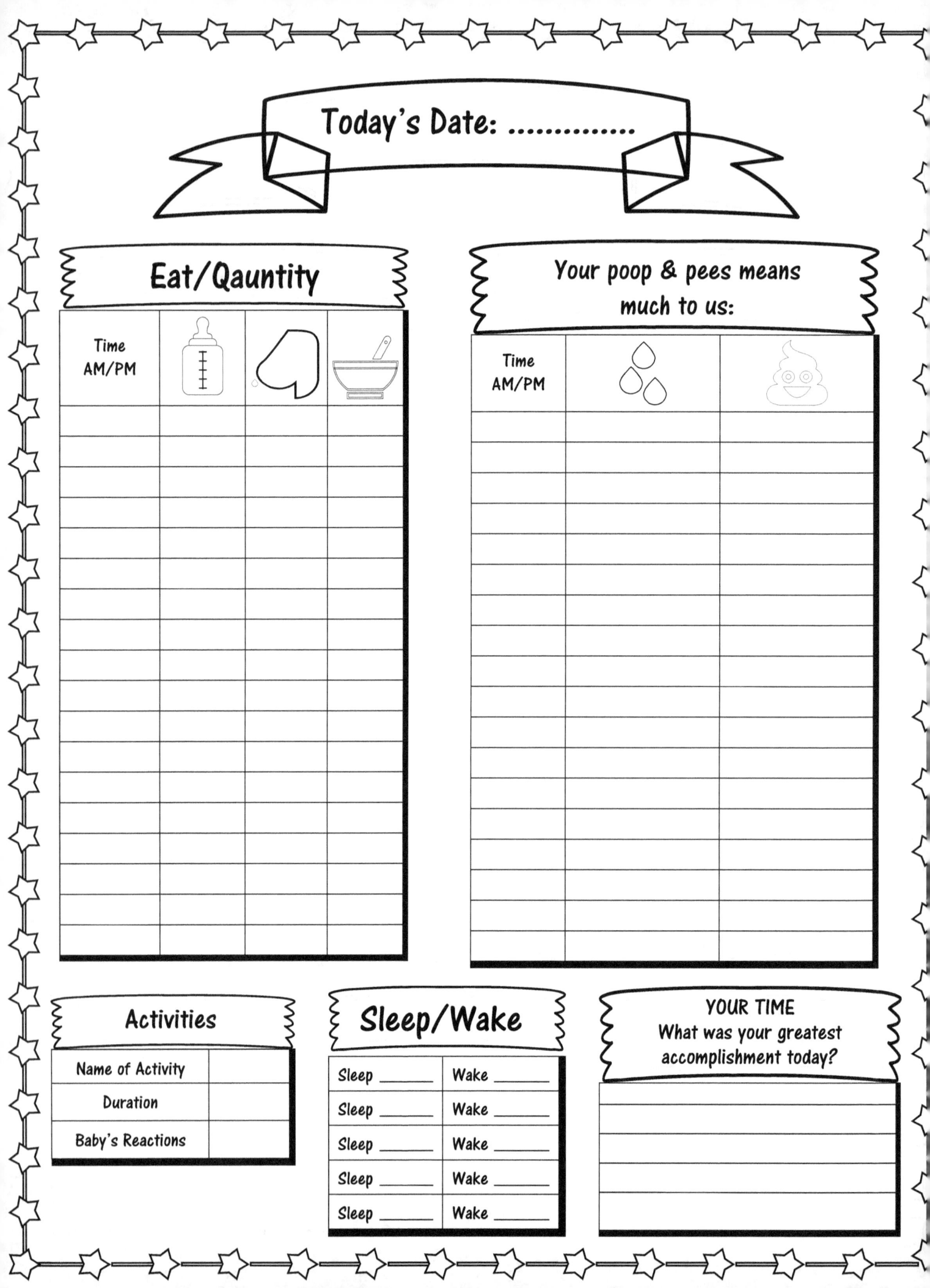

Today's Date: ....

Eat/Qauntity

Time AM/PM	🍼	🥛	🥣

Your poop & pees means much to us:

Time AM/PM	💧	💩

Activities

Name of Activity	
Duration	
Baby's Reactions	

Sleep/Wake

Sleep _____ Wake _____
Sleep _____ Wake _____
Sleep _____ Wake _____
Sleep _____ Wake _____
Sleep _____ Wake _____

YOUR TIME
What was your greatest accomplishment today?

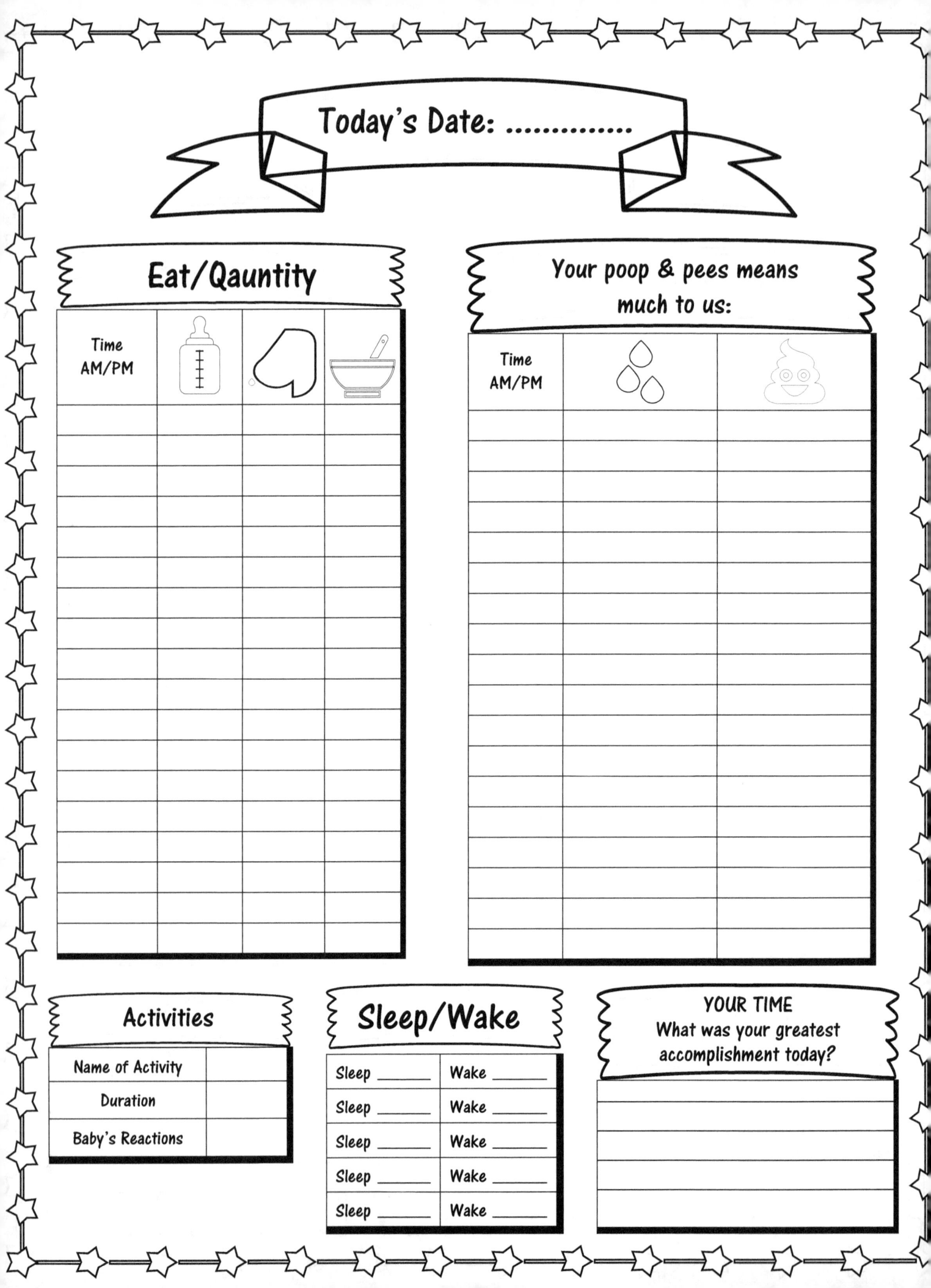

Today's Date: ....

Eat/Qauntity

Time AM/PM	🍼	💧	🥣

Your poop & pees means much to us:

Time AM/PM	💧	💩

Activities

Name of Activity	
Duration	
Baby's Reactions	

Sleep/Wake

Sleep _____   Wake _____
Sleep _____   Wake _____
Sleep _____   Wake _____
Sleep _____   Wake _____
Sleep _____   Wake _____

YOUR TIME
What was your greatest accomplishment today?

Today's Date: ....

Eat/Qauntity

Time AM/PM	🍼	🥛	🥣

Your poop & pees means much to us:

Time AM/PM	💧	💩

Activities

Name of Activity	
Duration	
Baby's Reactions	

Sleep/Wake

Sleep _____ Wake _____

Sleep _____ Wake _____

Sleep _____ Wake _____

Sleep _____ Wake _____

Sleep _____ Wake _____

YOUR TIME
What was your greatest accomplishment today?

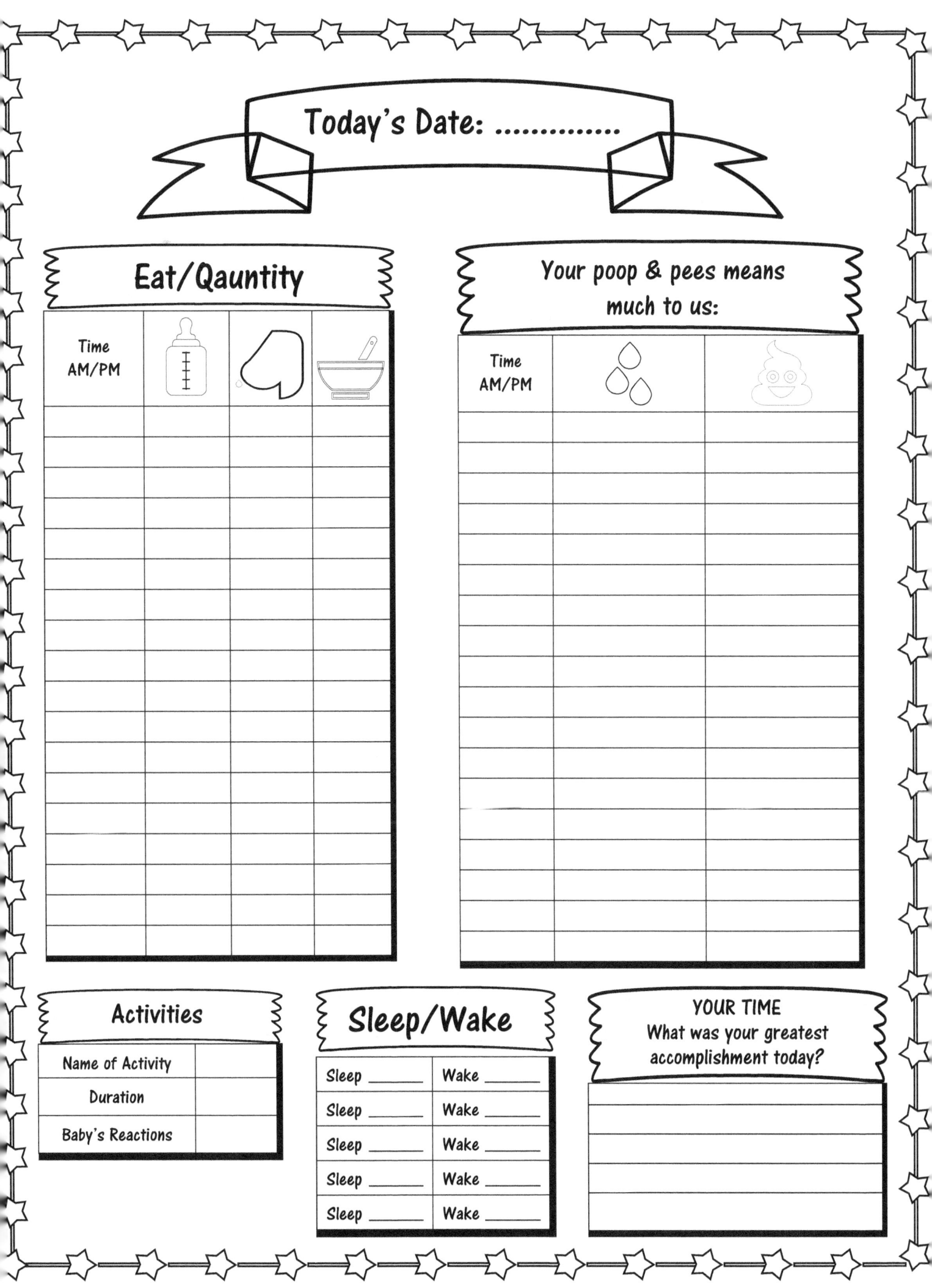

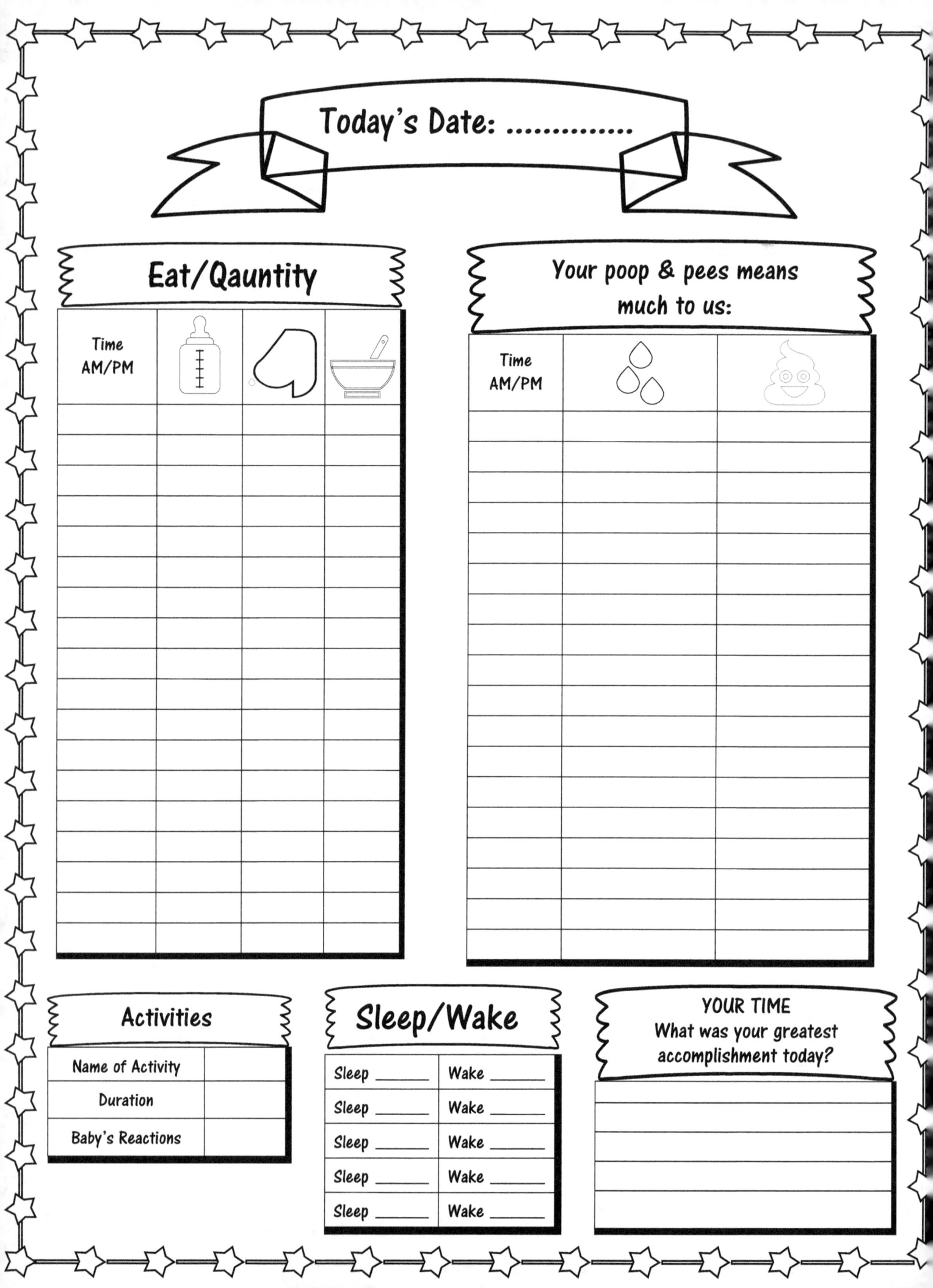

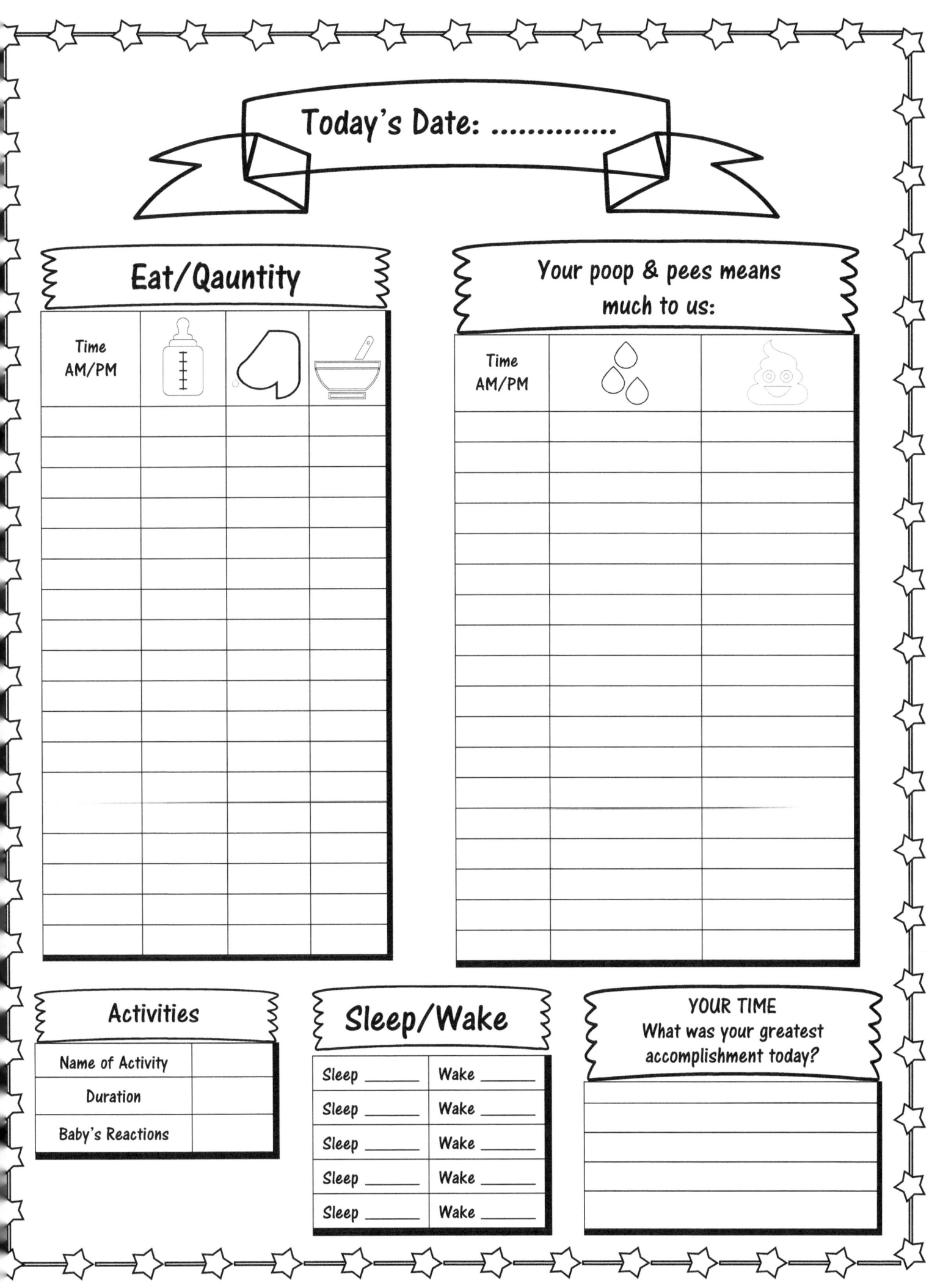

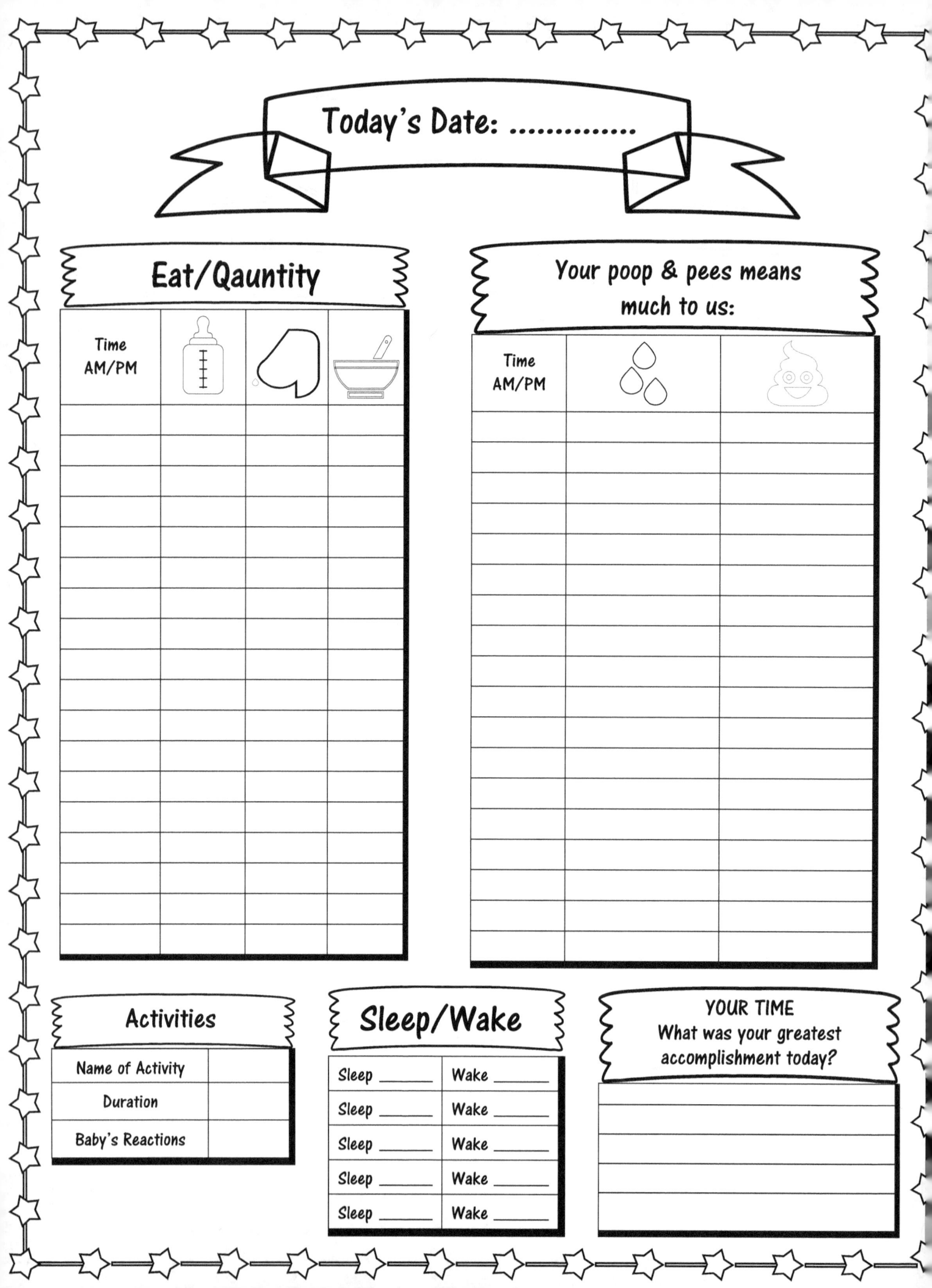

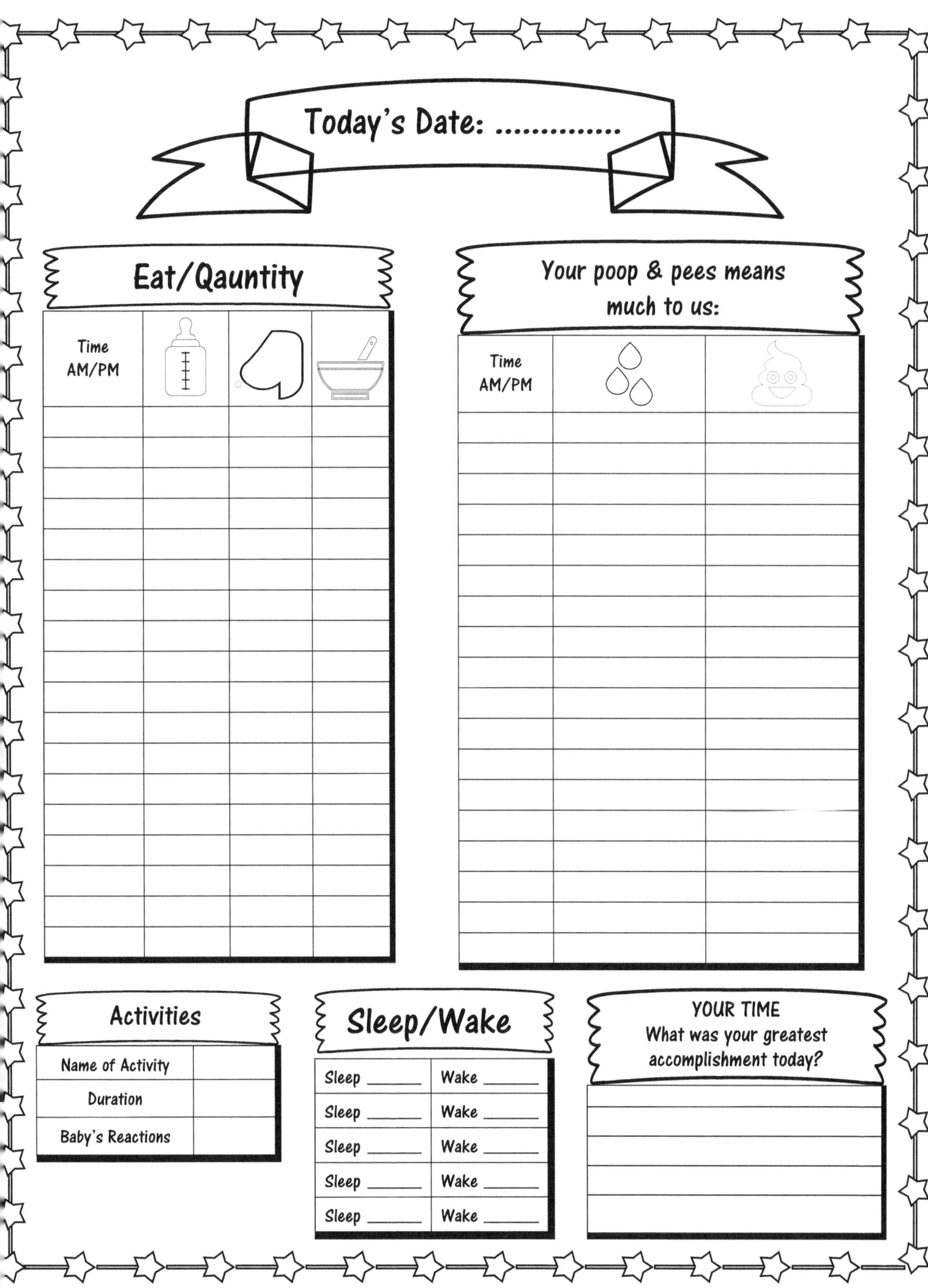

Today's Date: ....

Eat/Qauntity

Time AM/PM			

Your poop & pees means much to us:

Time AM/PM		

Activities

Name of Activity	
Duration	
Baby's Reactions	

Sleep/Wake

Sleep _____ Wake _____

Sleep _____ Wake _____

Sleep _____ Wake _____

Sleep _____ Wake _____

Sleep _____ Wake _____

YOUR TIME
What was your greatest accomplishment today?

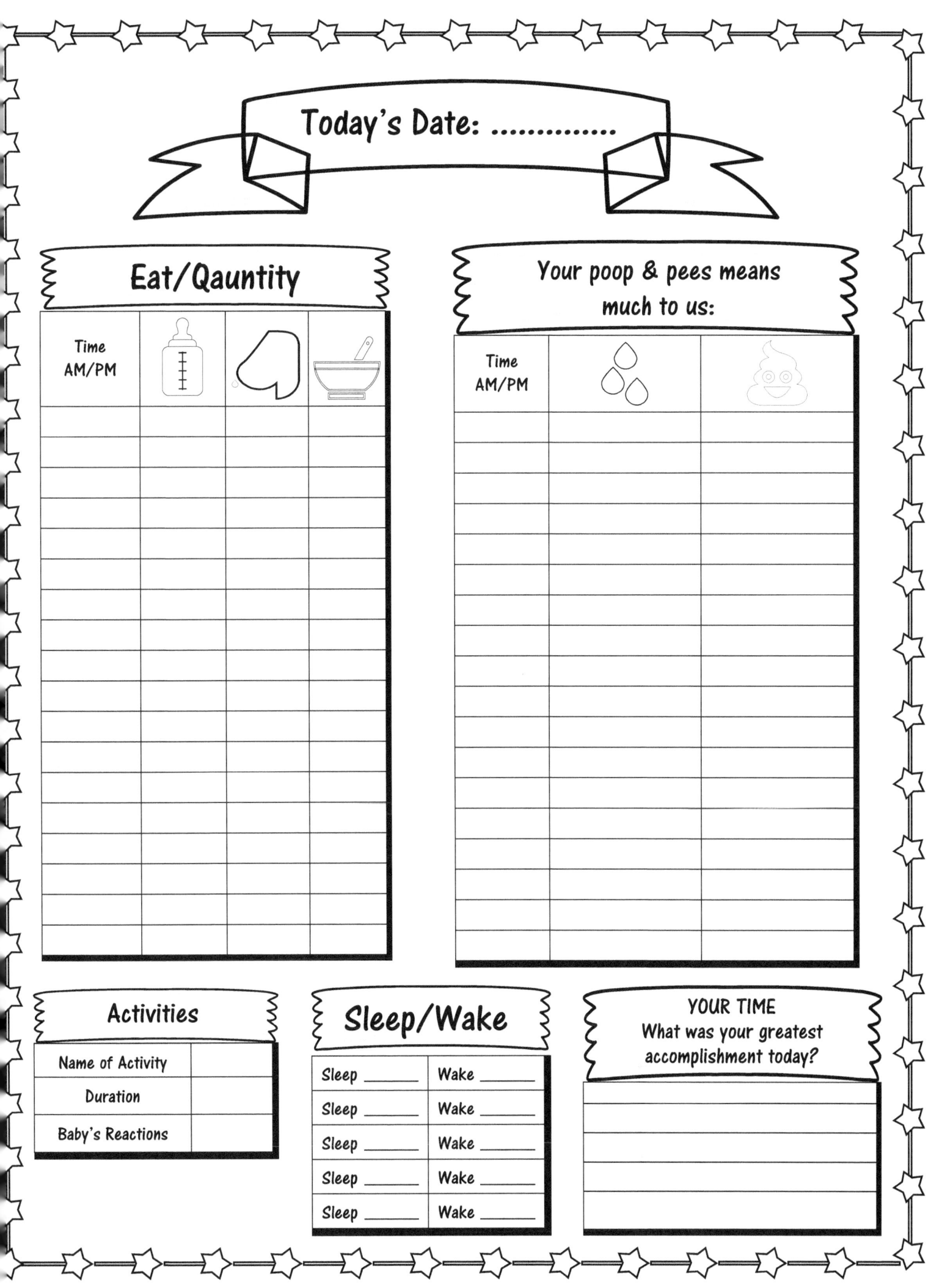

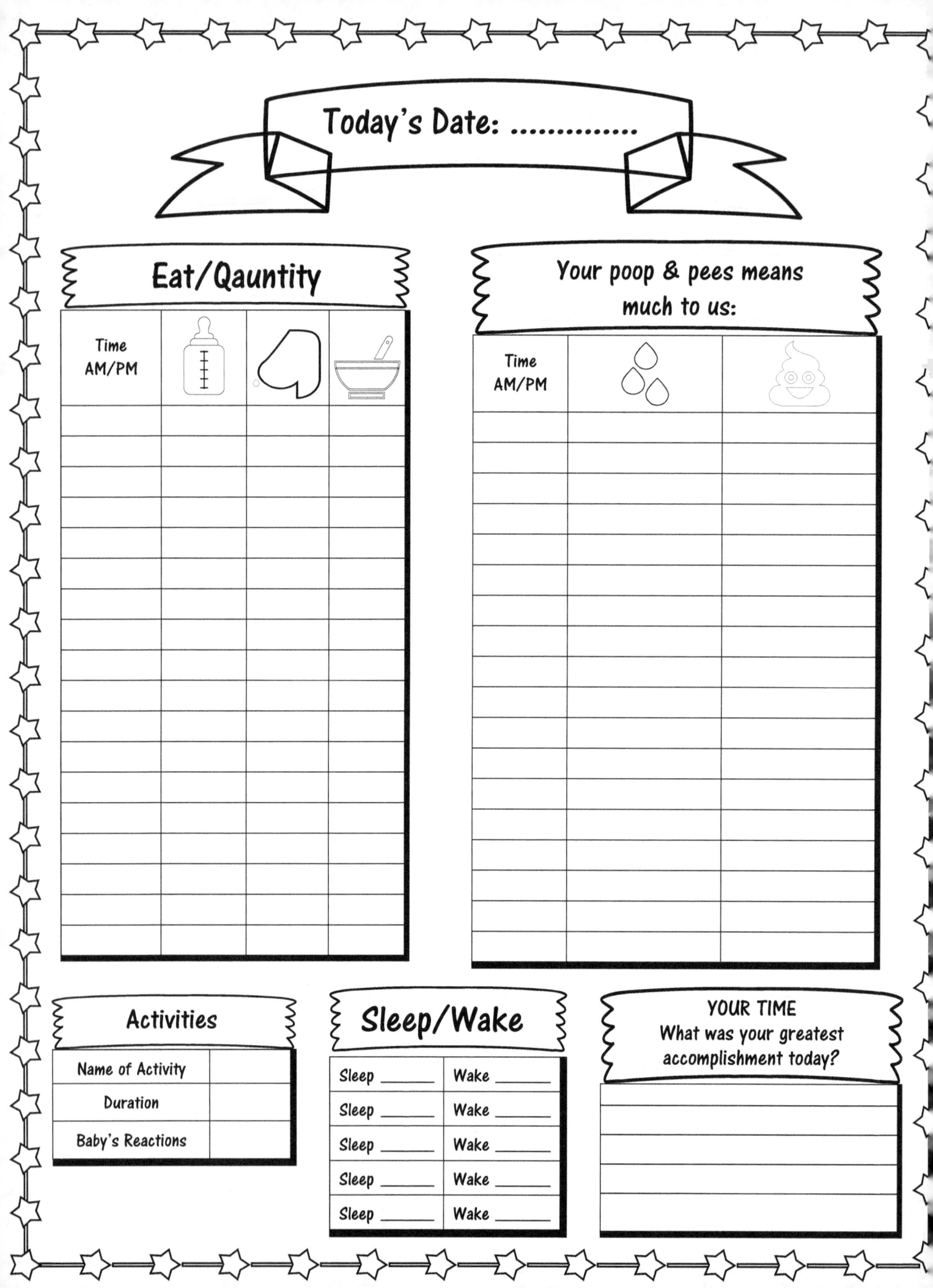

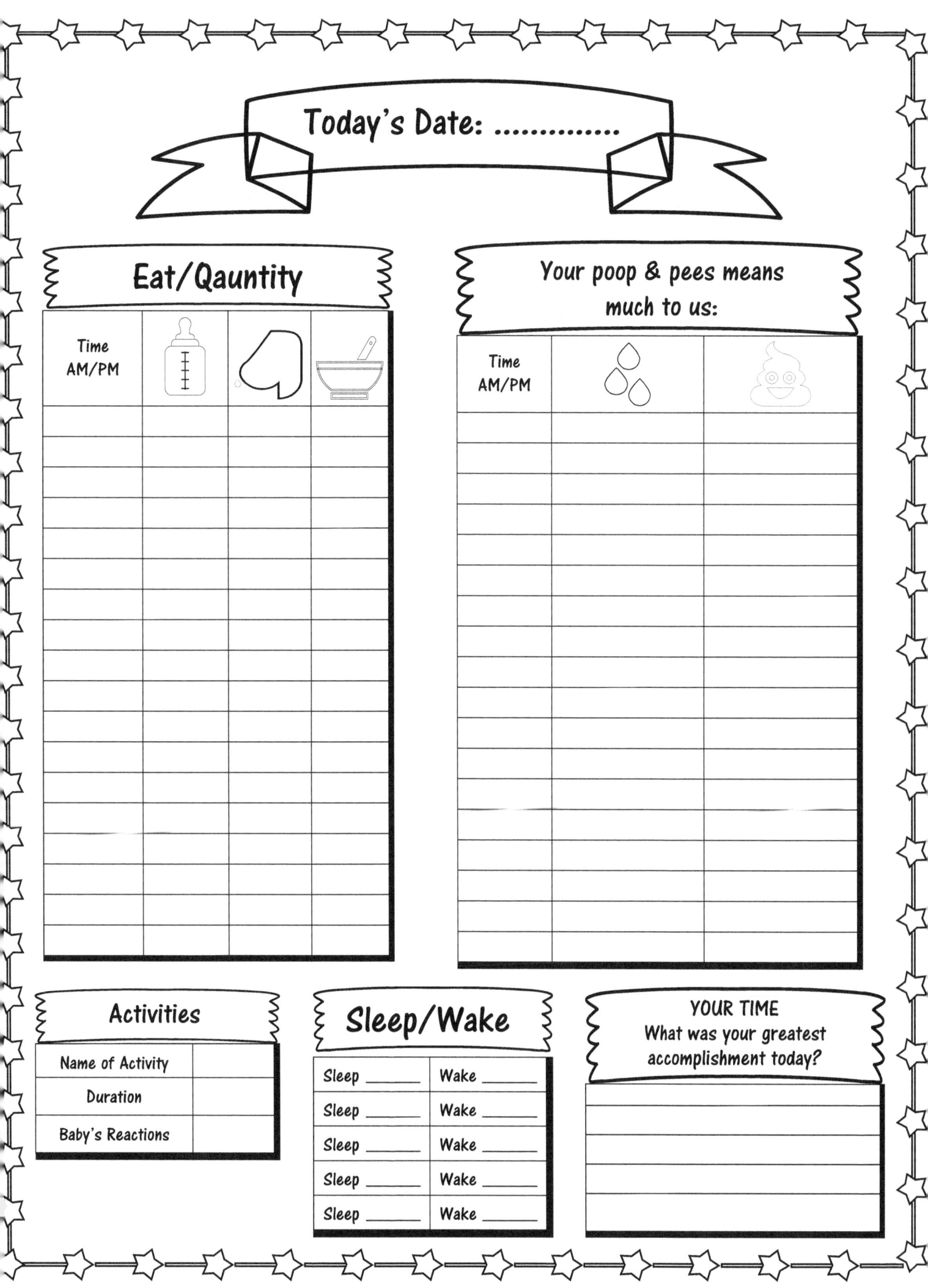

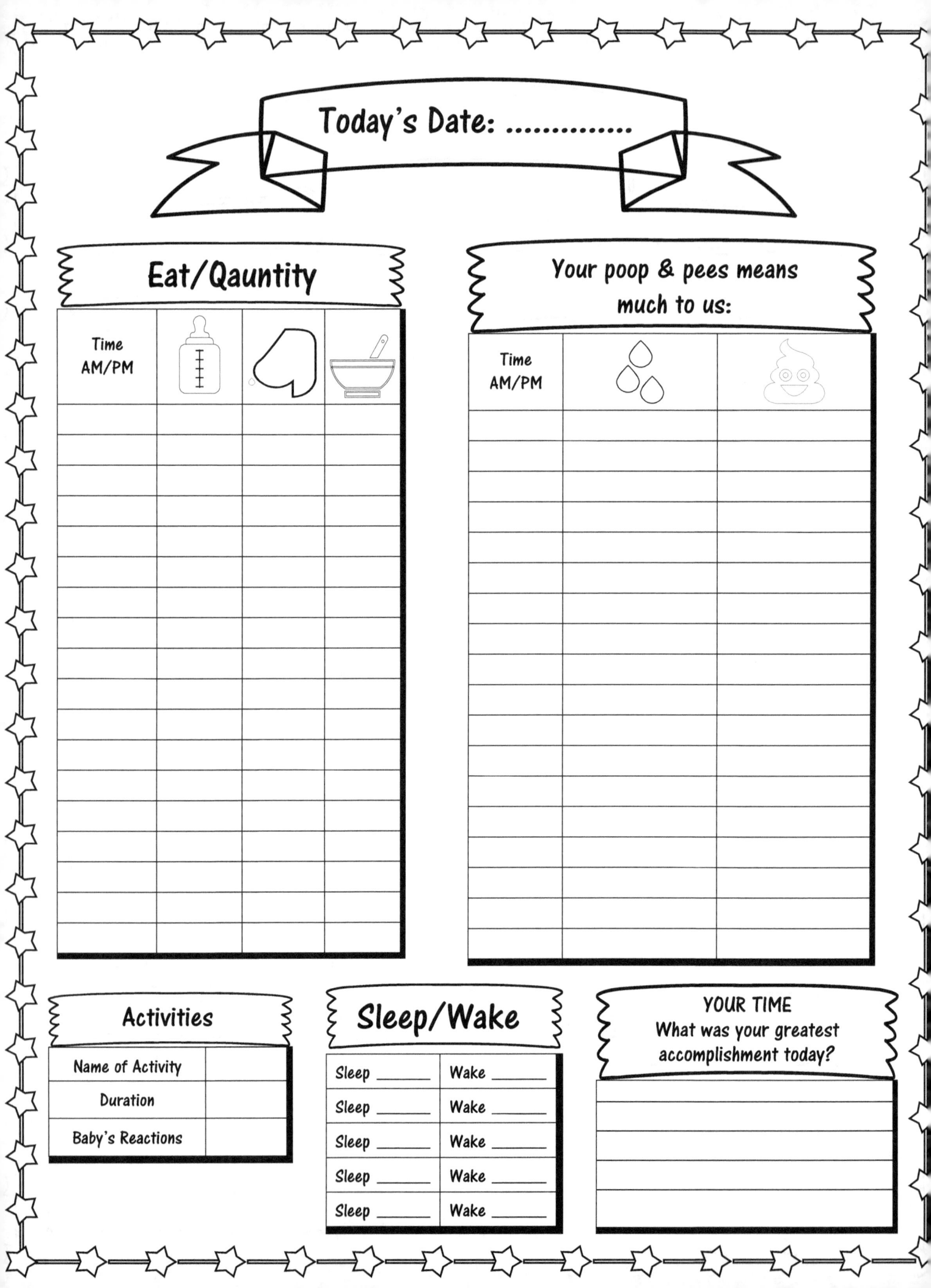

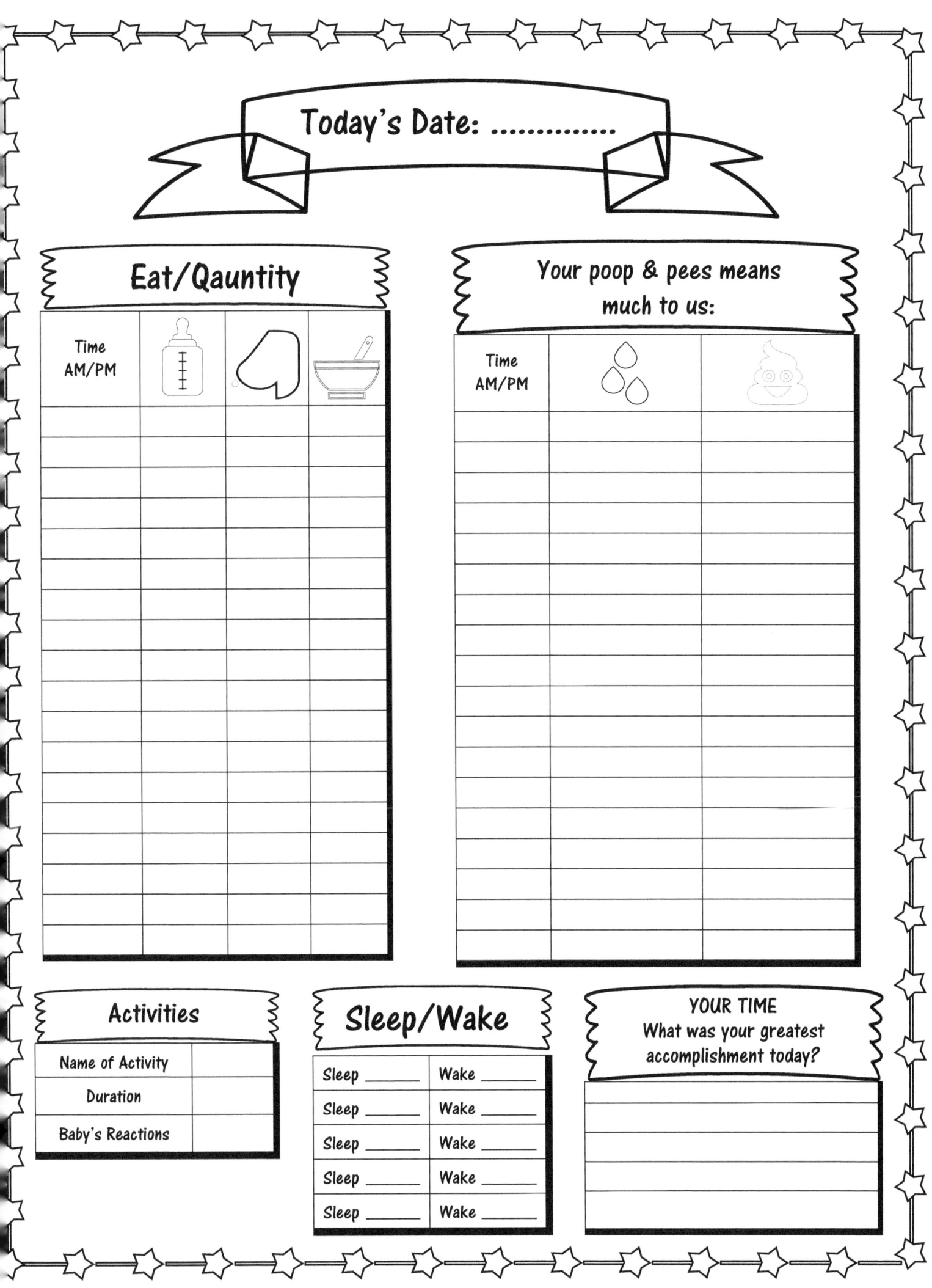

Today's Date: ....

Eat/Qauntity

Time AM/PM	🍼	🤱	🥣

Your poop & pees means much to us:

Time AM/PM	💧	💩

Activities

Name of Activity	
Duration	
Baby's Reactions	

Sleep/Wake

Sleep _____ Wake _____
Sleep _____ Wake _____
Sleep _____ Wake _____
Sleep _____ Wake _____
Sleep _____ Wake _____

YOUR TIME
What was your greatest accomplishment today?

Today's Date: ....

Eat/Qauntity

Time AM/PM	🍼	🤱	🥣

Your poop & pees means much to us:

Time AM/PM	💧	💩

Activities

Name of Activity	
Duration	
Baby's Reactions	

Sleep/Wake

Sleep _____	Wake _____
Sleep _____	Wake _____
Sleep _____	Wake _____
Sleep _____	Wake _____
Sleep _____	Wake _____

YOUR TIME
What was your greatest accomplishment today?

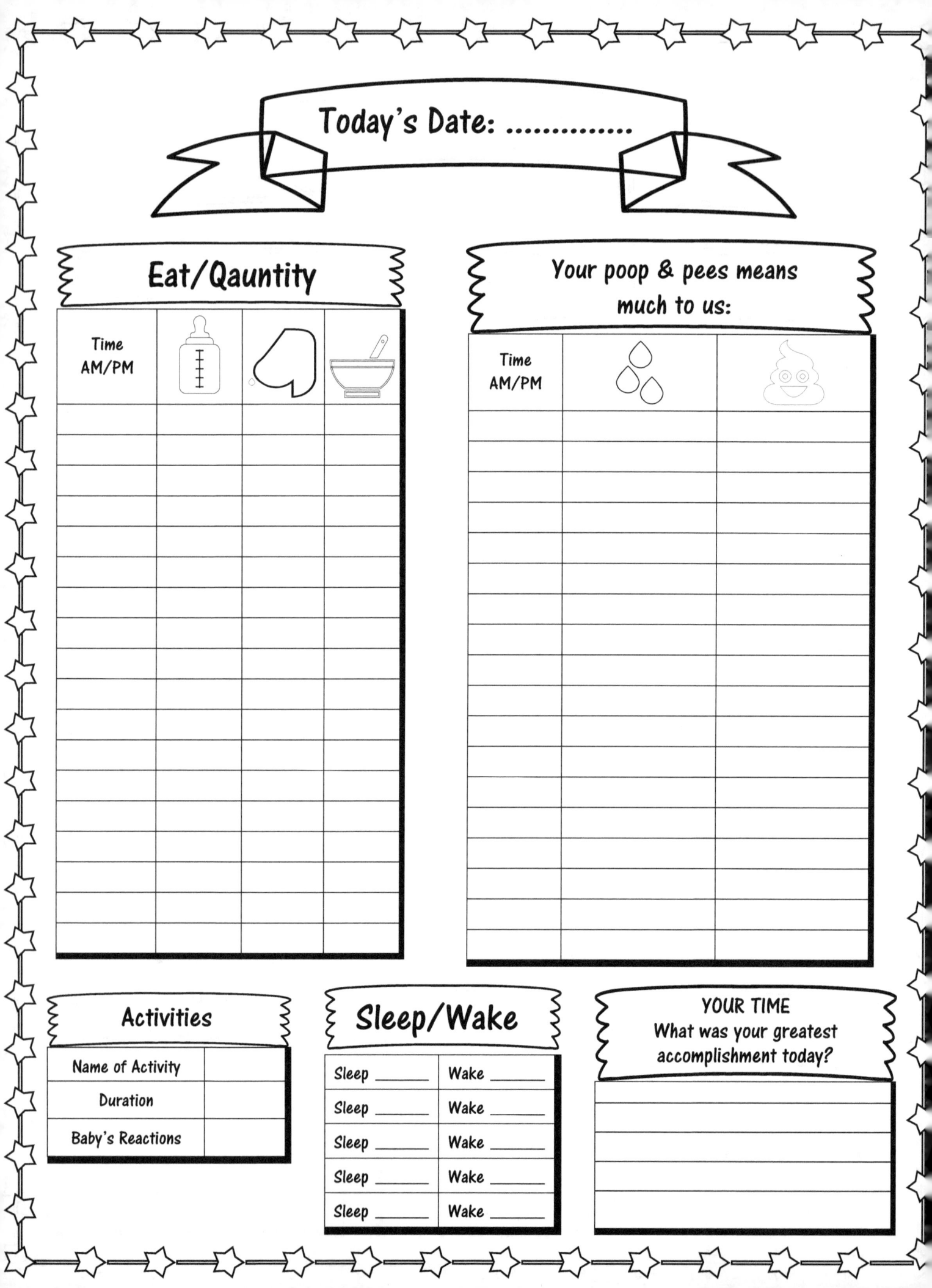

Today's Date: ....

Eat/Qauntity

Time AM/PM	🍼	🤱	🥣

Your poop & pees means much to us:

Time AM/PM	💧	💩

Activities

Name of Activity	
Duration	
Baby's Reactions	

Sleep/Wake

Sleep _____ Wake _____
Sleep _____ Wake _____
Sleep _____ Wake _____
Sleep _____ Wake _____
Sleep _____ Wake _____

YOUR TIME
What was your greatest accomplishment today?

Today's Date: ....

Eat/Qauntity

Time AM/PM	🍼	🤱	🥣

Your poop & pees means much to us:

Time AM/PM	💧	💩

Activities

Name of Activity	
Duration	
Baby's Reactions	

Sleep/Wake

Sleep _____ Wake _____
Sleep _____ Wake _____
Sleep _____ Wake _____
Sleep _____ Wake _____
Sleep _____ Wake _____

YOUR TIME
What was your greatest accomplishment today?

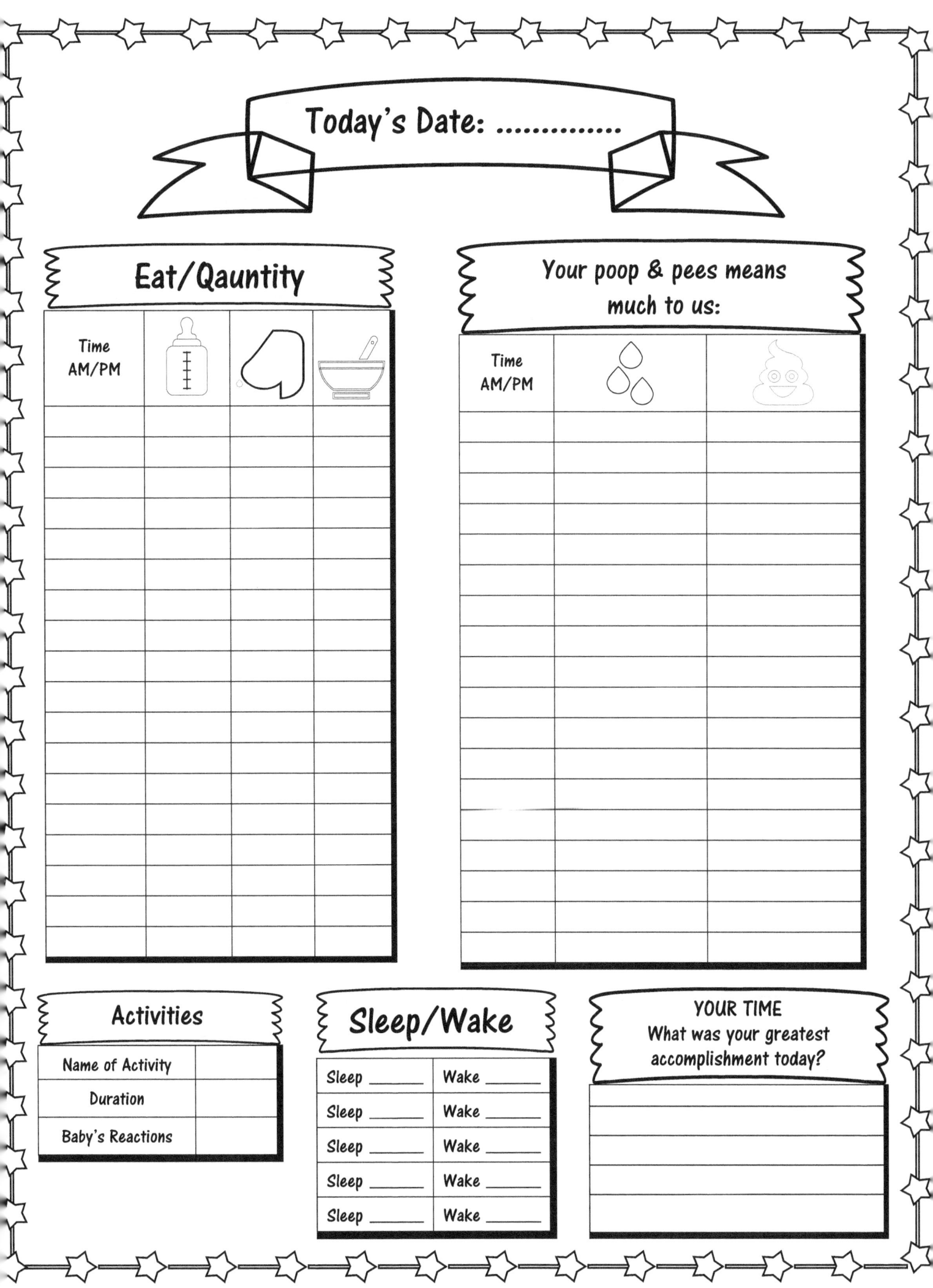

Today's Date: ....

Eat/Qauntity

Time AM/PM	🍼	🤱	🥣

Your poop & pees means much to us:

Time AM/PM	💧	💩

Activities

Name of Activity	
Duration	
Baby's Reactions	

Sleep/Wake

Sleep _____ Wake _____

Sleep _____ Wake _____

Sleep _____ Wake _____

Sleep _____ Wake _____

Sleep _____ Wake _____

YOUR TIME
What was your greatest accomplishment today?

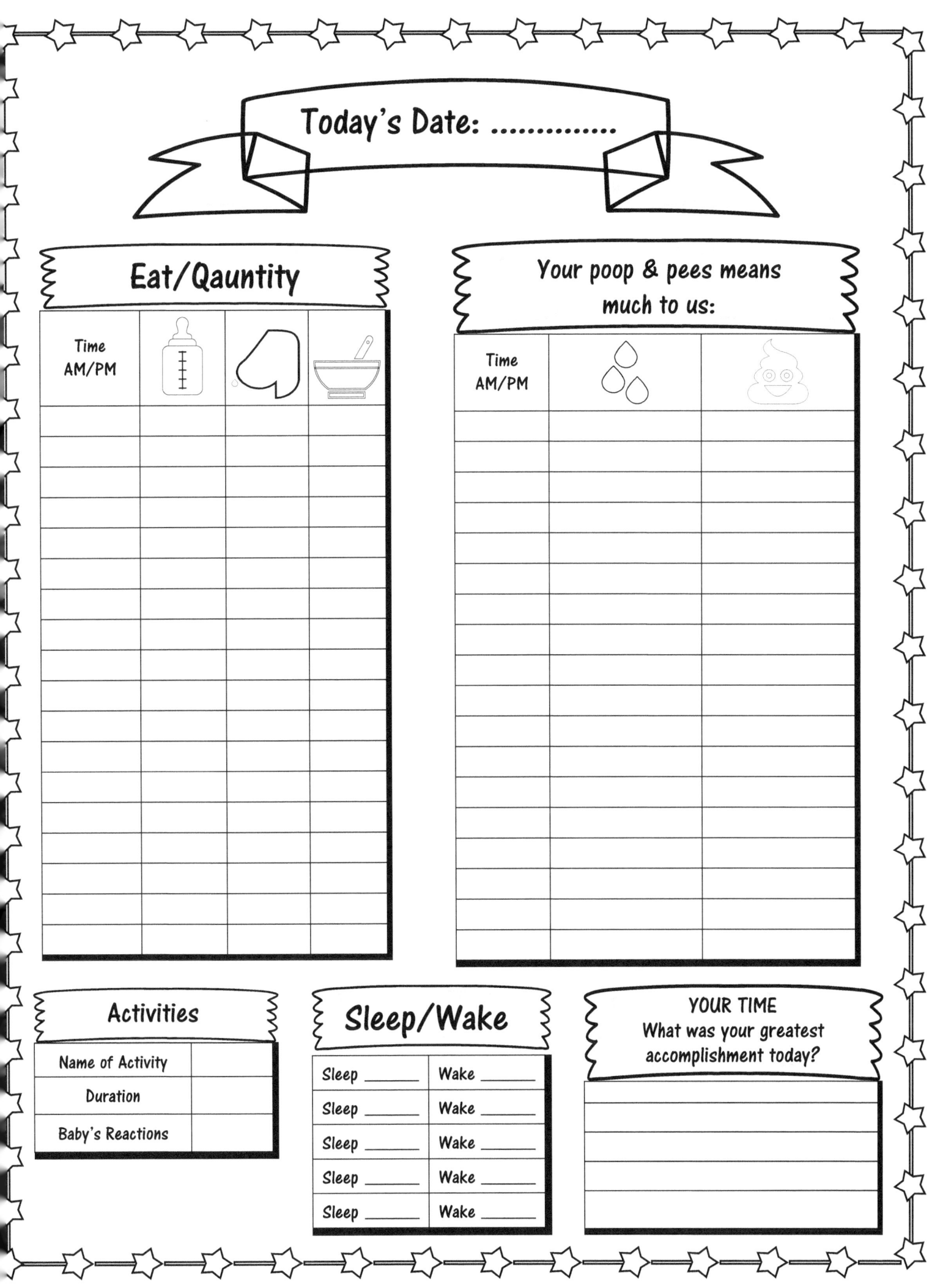

Today's Date: ....

Eat/Qauntity

Time AM/PM	🍼	🤱	🥣

Your poop & pees means much to us:

Time AM/PM	💧	💩

Activities

Name of Activity	
Duration	
Baby's Reactions	

Sleep/Wake

Sleep _____ Wake _____

Sleep _____ Wake _____

Sleep _____ Wake _____

Sleep _____ Wake _____

Sleep _____ Wake _____

YOUR TIME
What was your greatest accomplishment today?

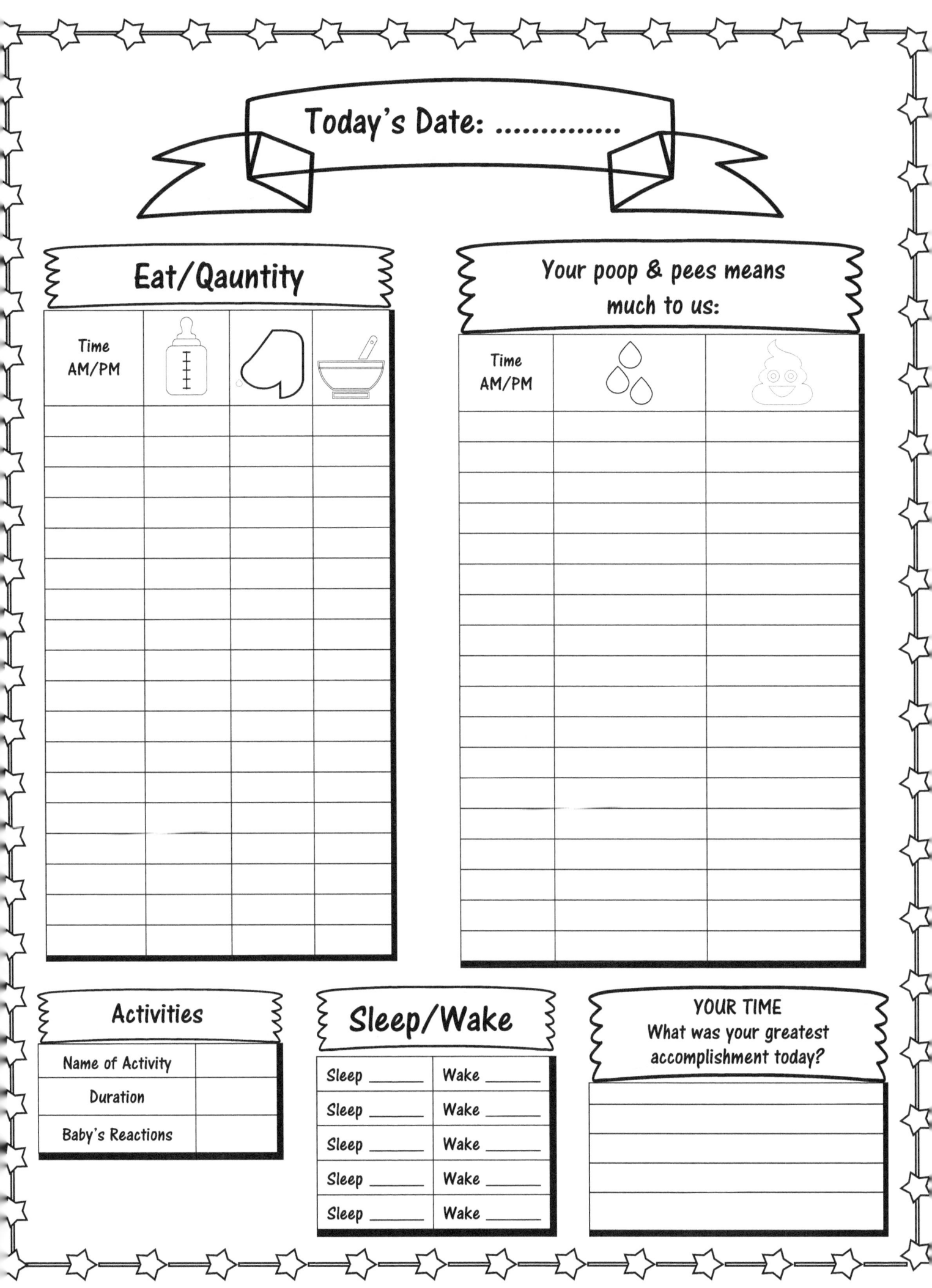

Today's Date: ....

Eat/Qauntity

Time AM/PM	🍼	🤱	🥣

Your poop & pees means much to us:

Time AM/PM	💧	💩

Activities

Name of Activity	
Duration	
Baby's Reactions	

Sleep/Wake

Sleep _____   Wake _____
Sleep _____   Wake _____
Sleep _____   Wake _____
Sleep _____   Wake _____
Sleep _____   Wake _____

YOUR TIME
What was your greatest accomplishment today?

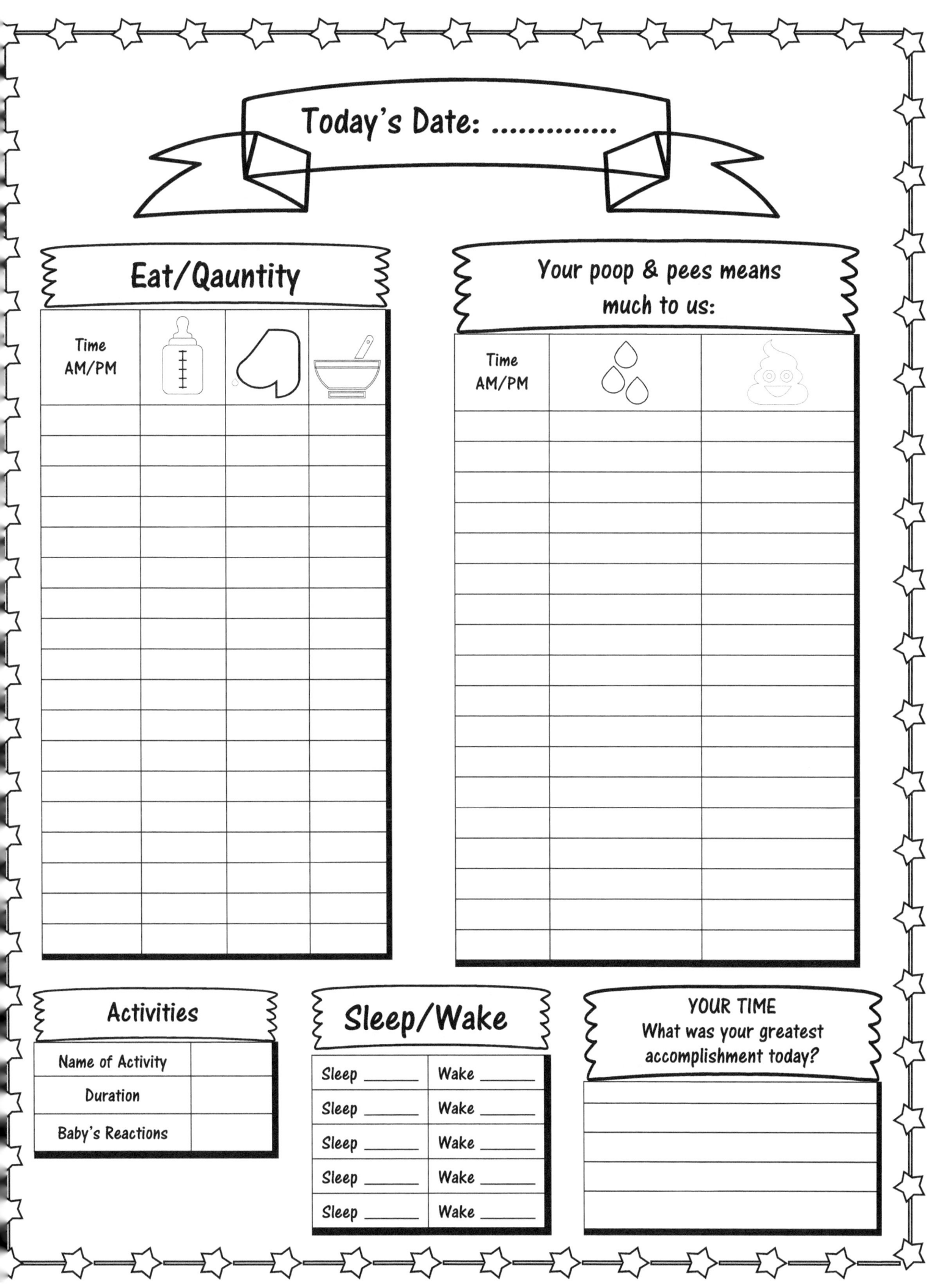

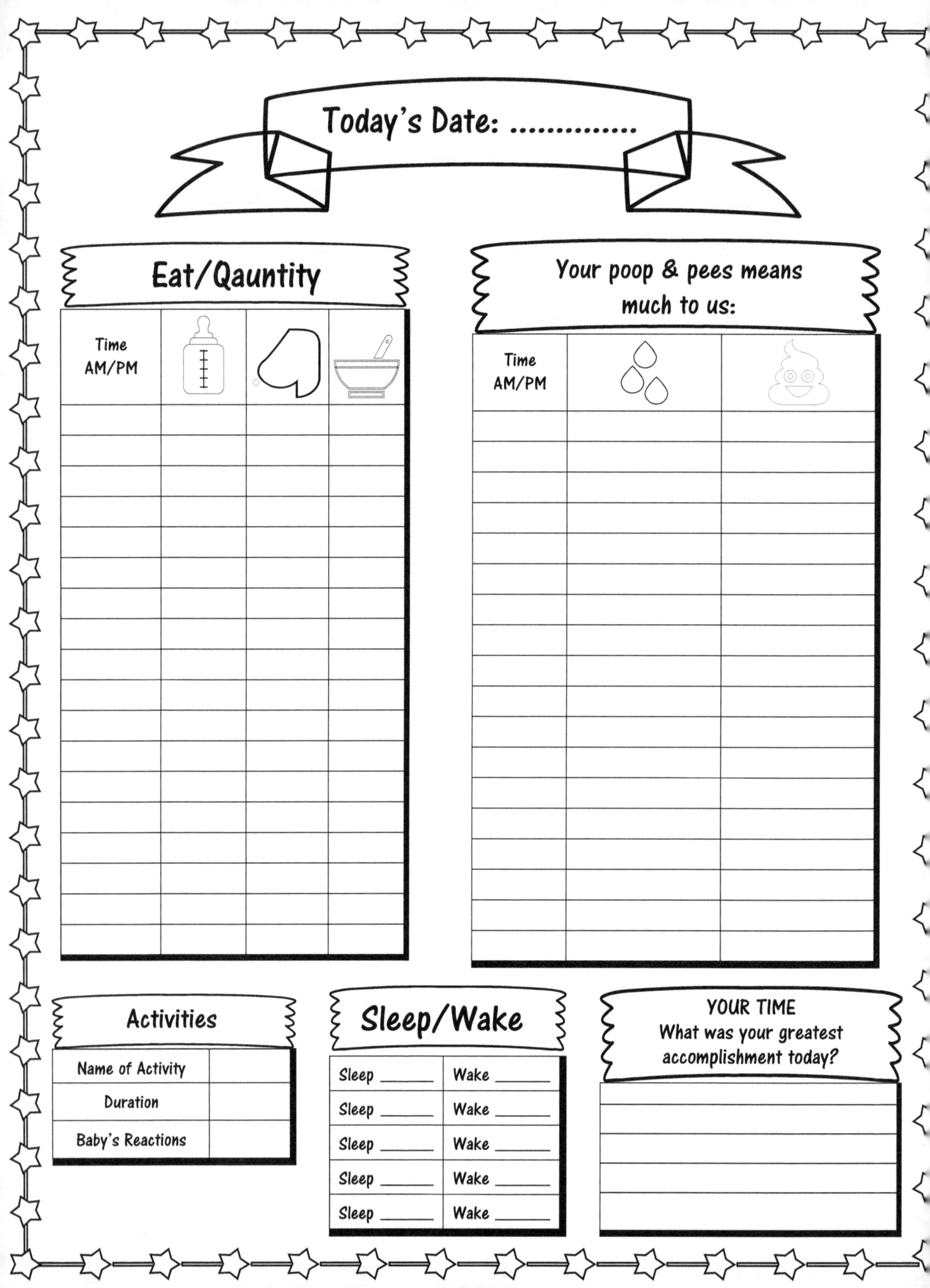

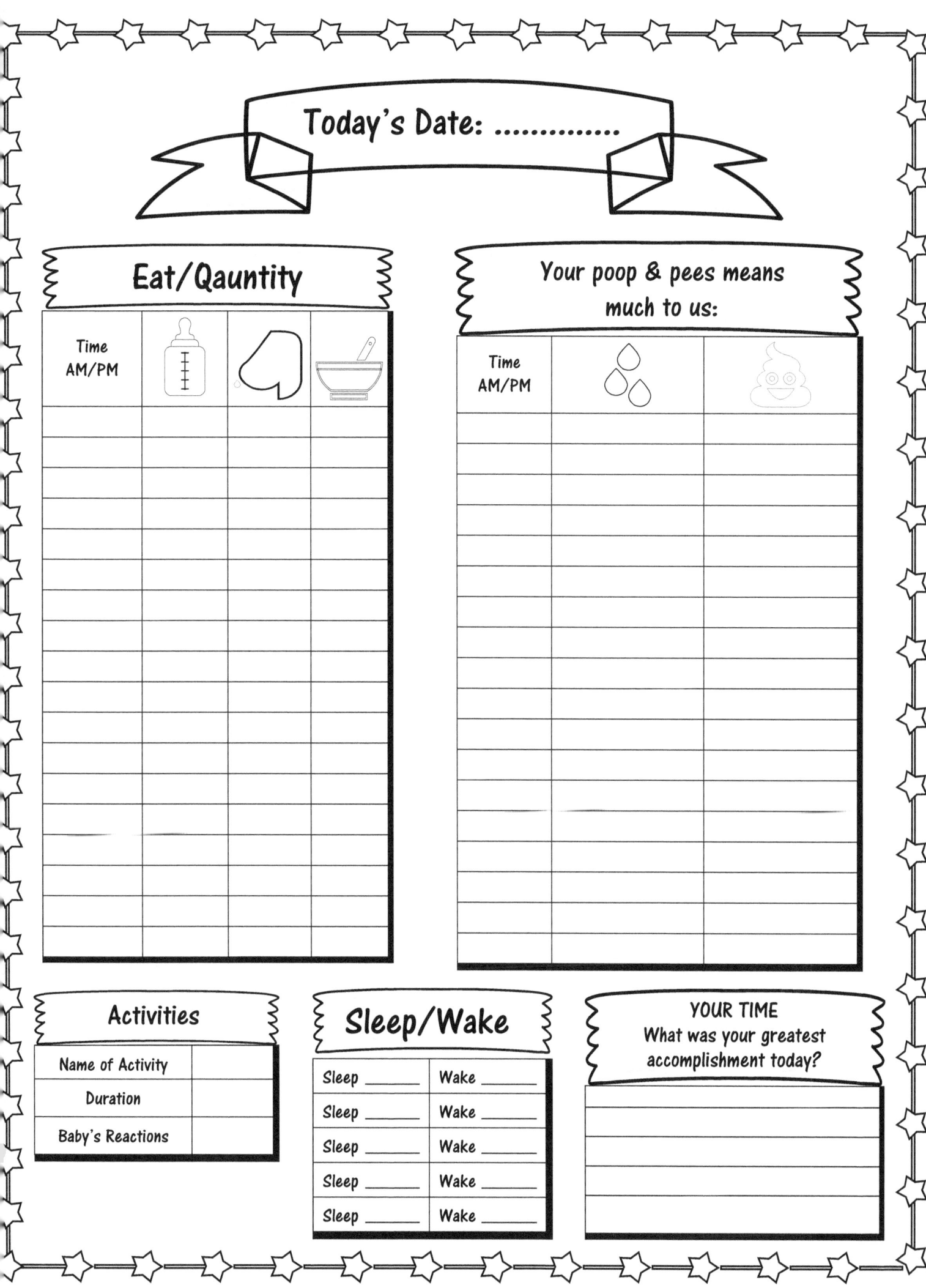

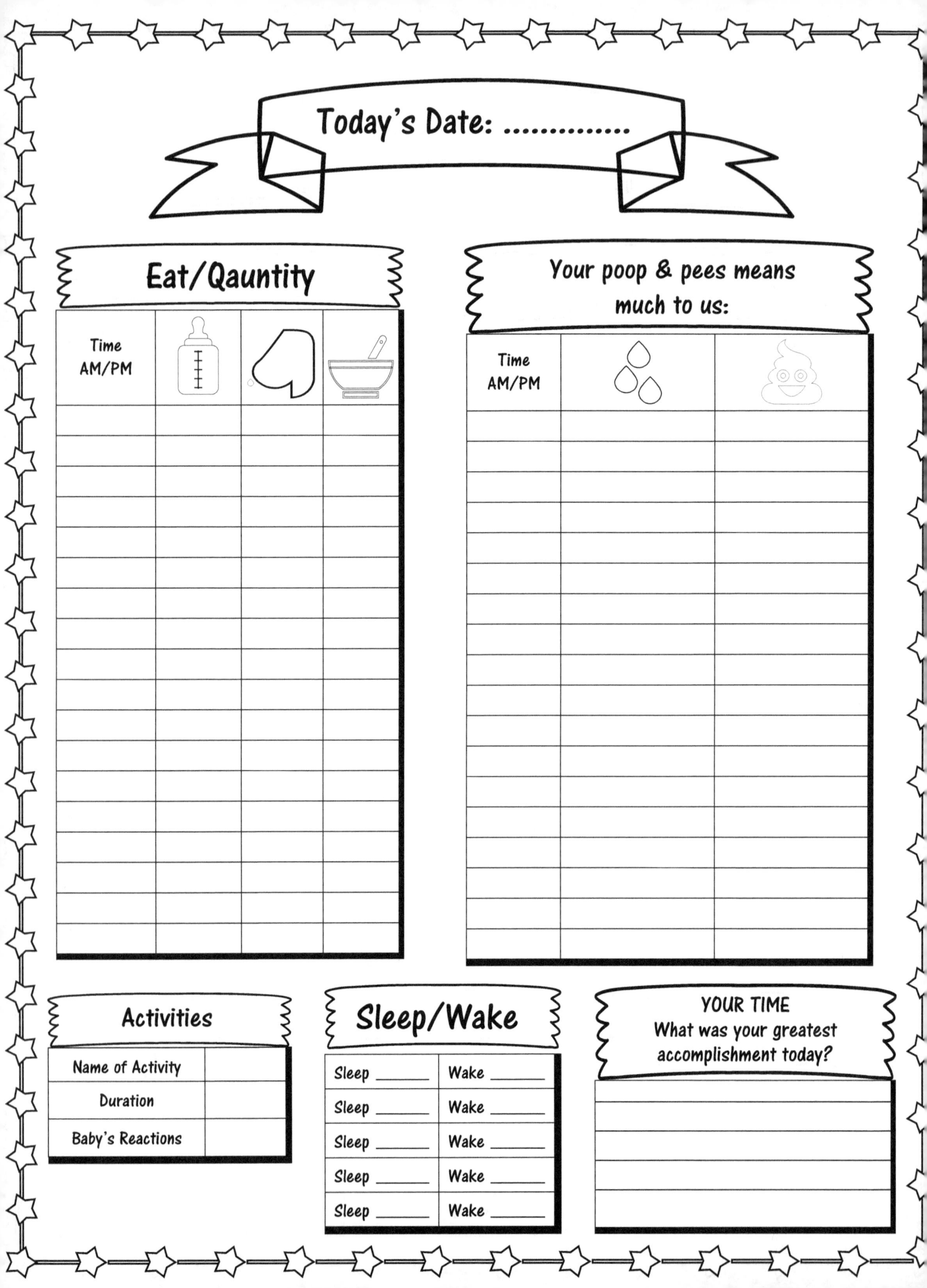

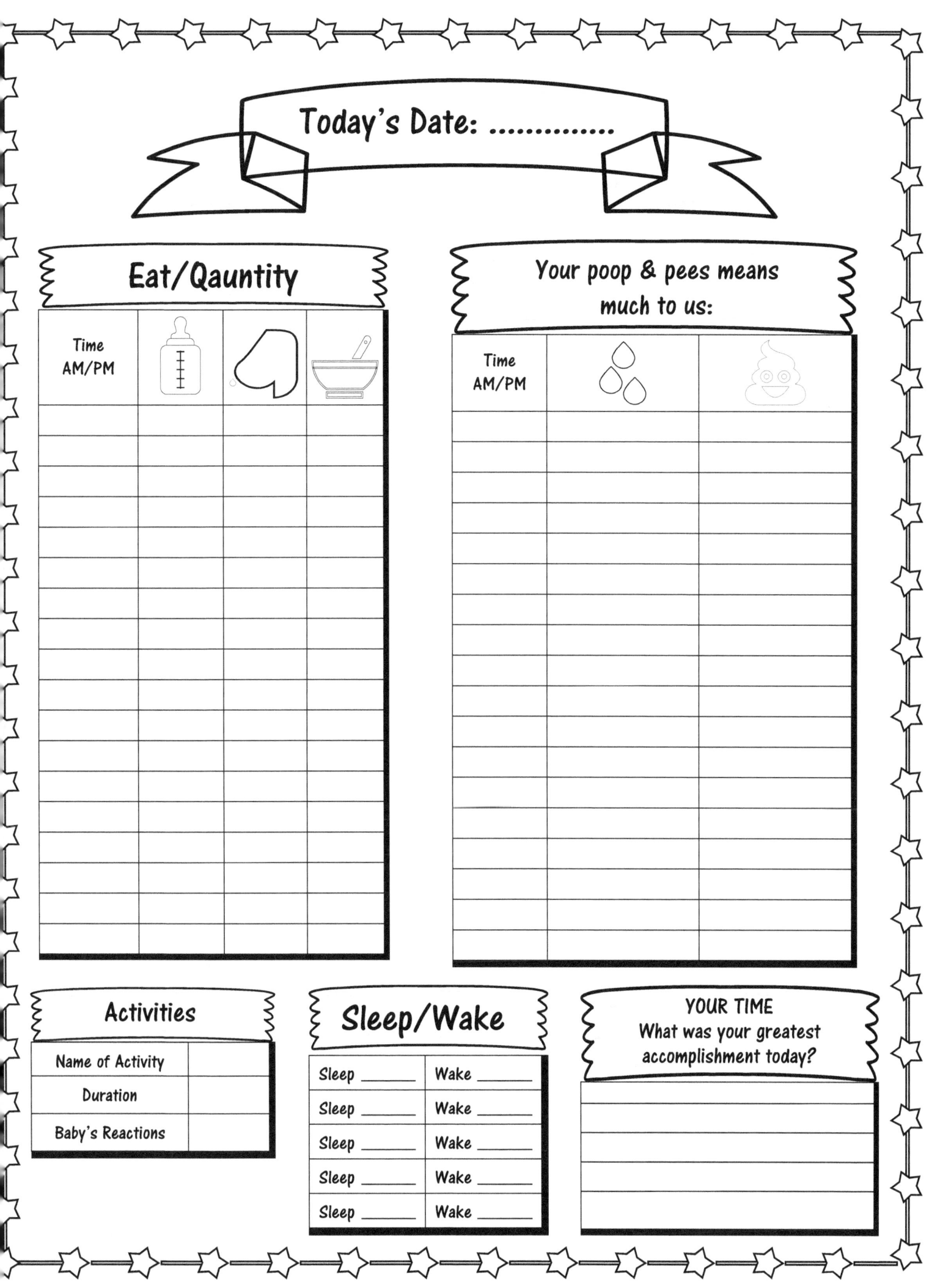

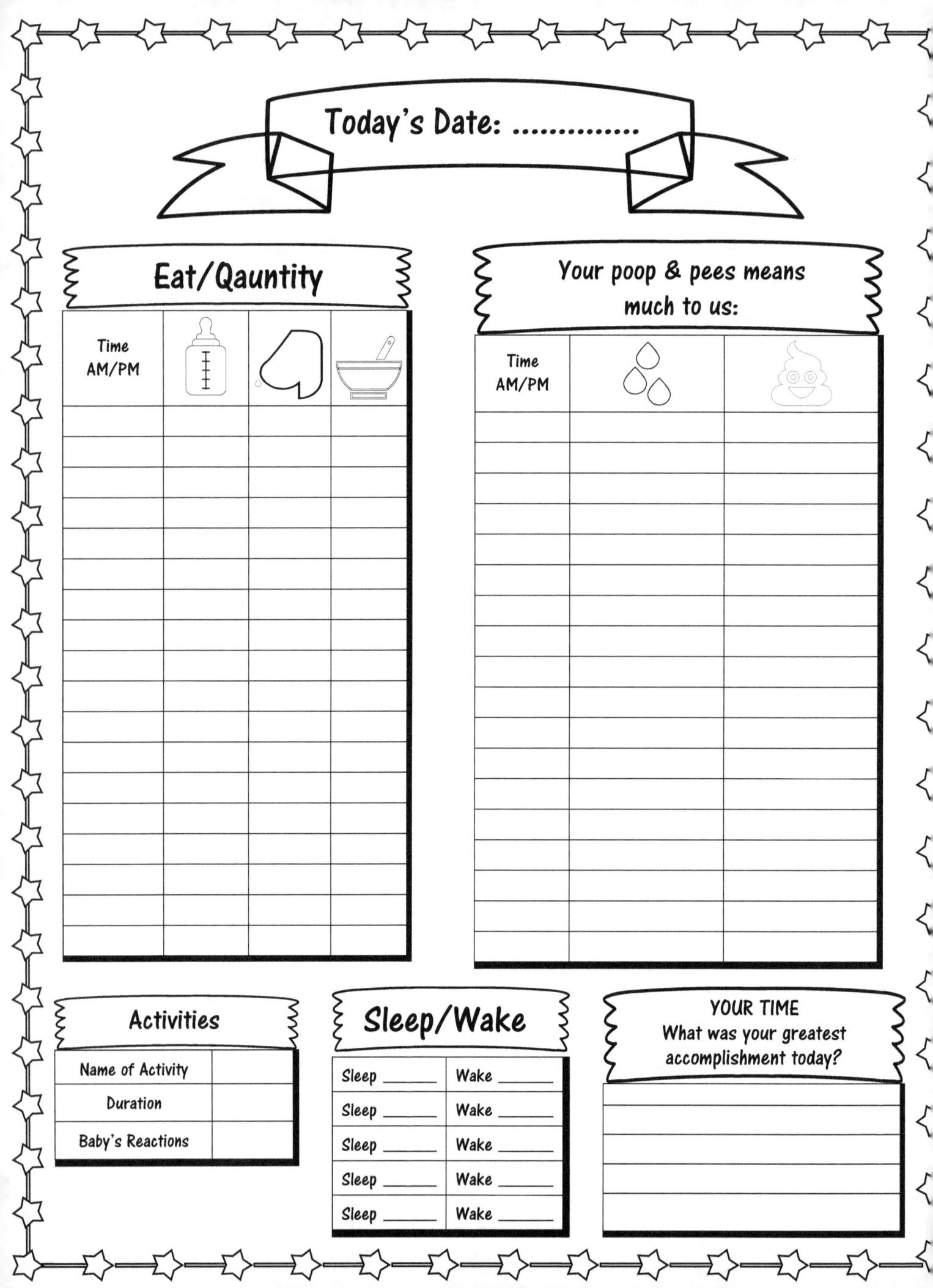

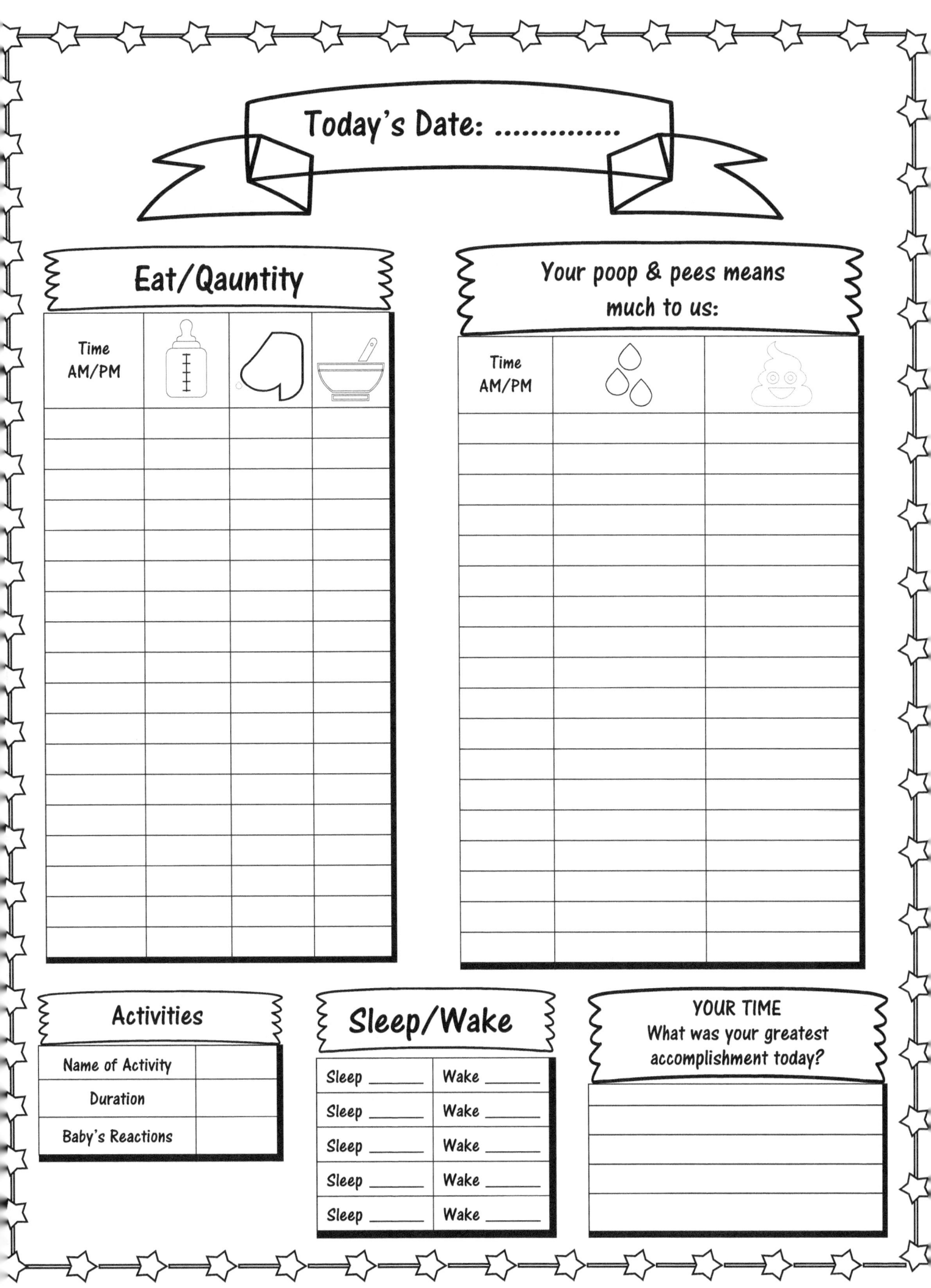

Today's Date: ....

Eat/Qauntity

Time AM/PM	🍼		🥣

Your poop & pees means much to us:

Time AM/PM	💧	💩

Activities

Name of Activity	
Duration	
Baby's Reactions	

Sleep/Wake

Sleep _____ Wake _____
Sleep _____ Wake _____
Sleep _____ Wake _____
Sleep _____ Wake _____
Sleep _____ Wake _____

YOUR TIME
What was your greatest accomplishment today?

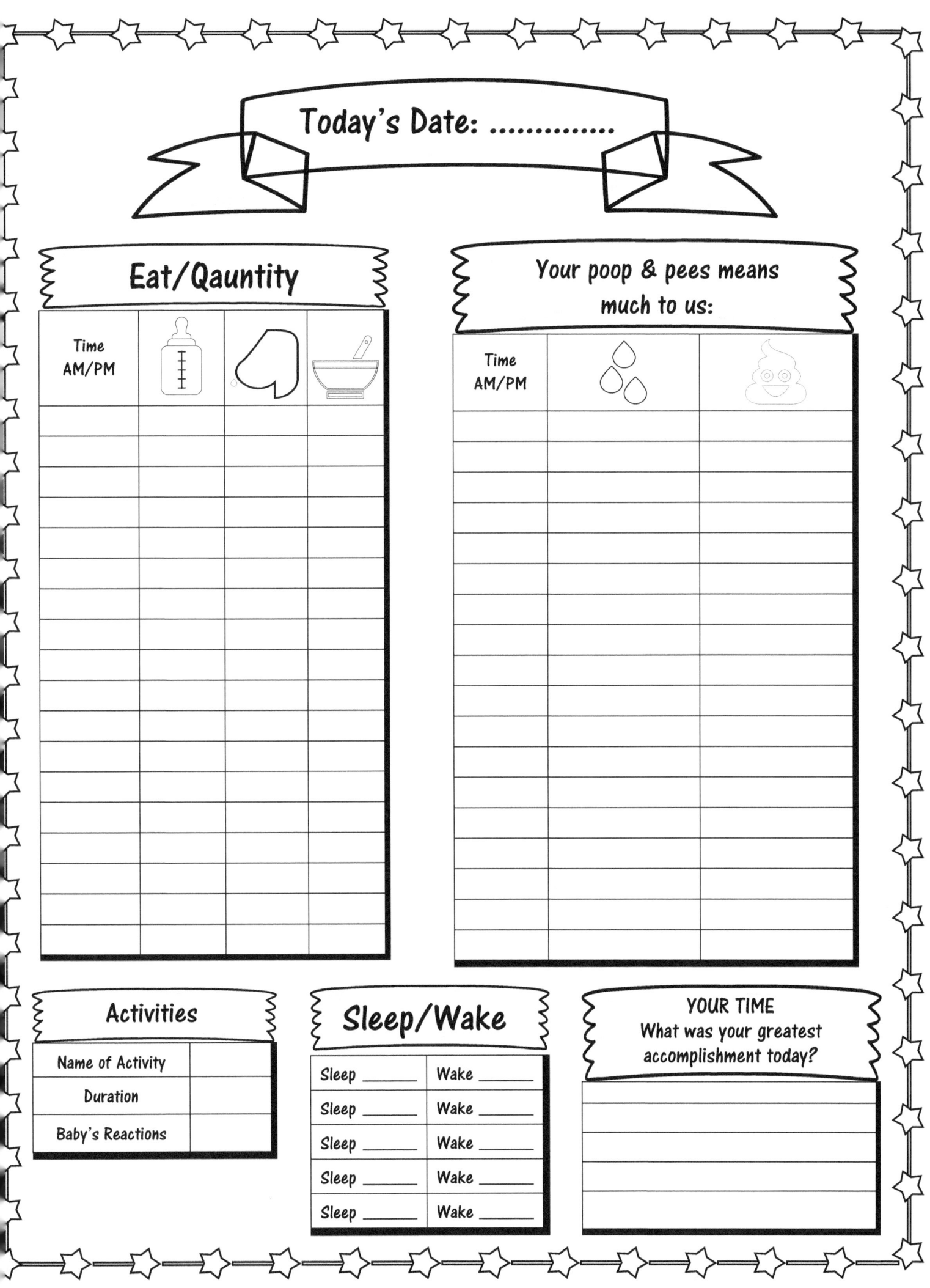

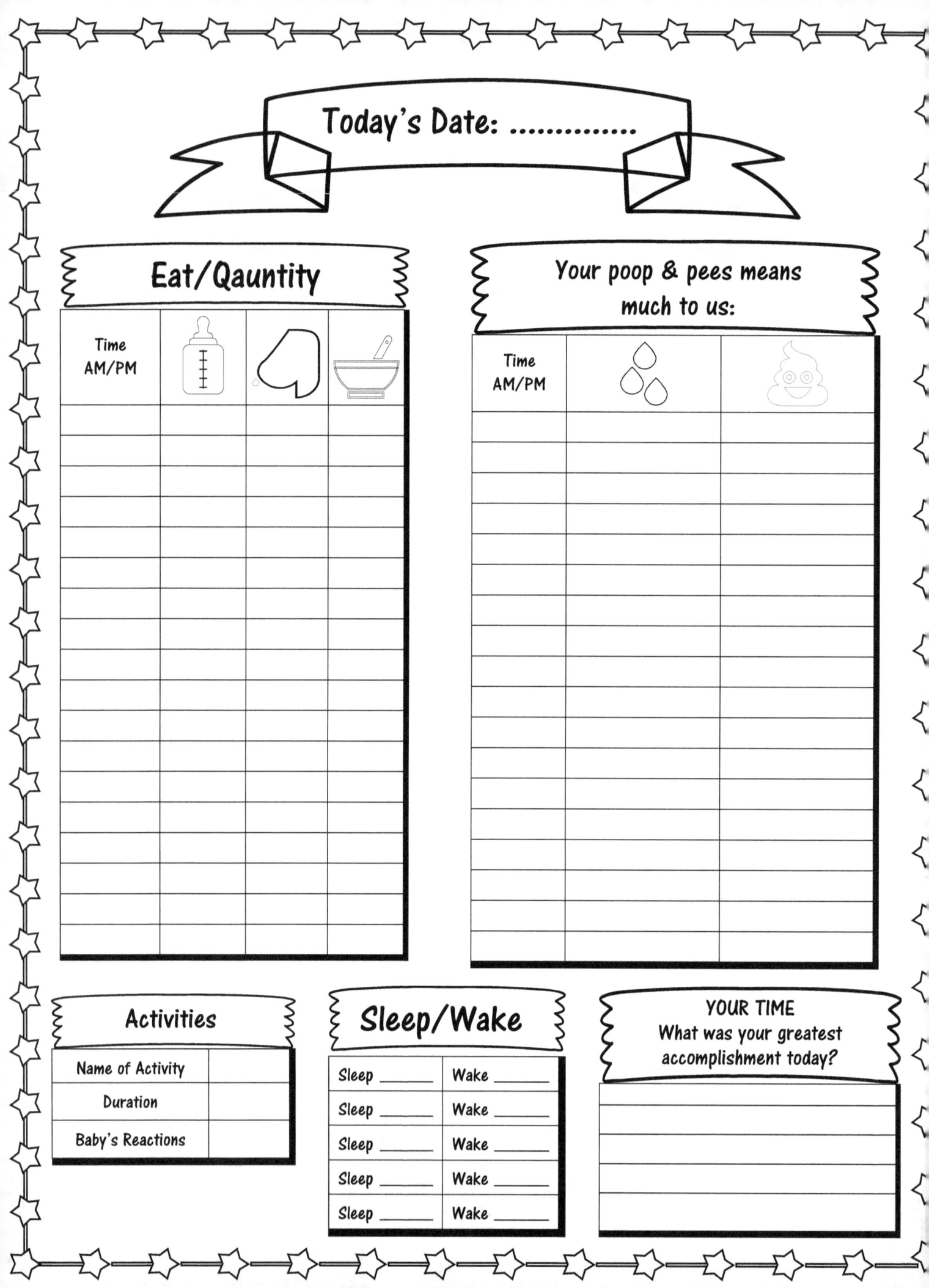

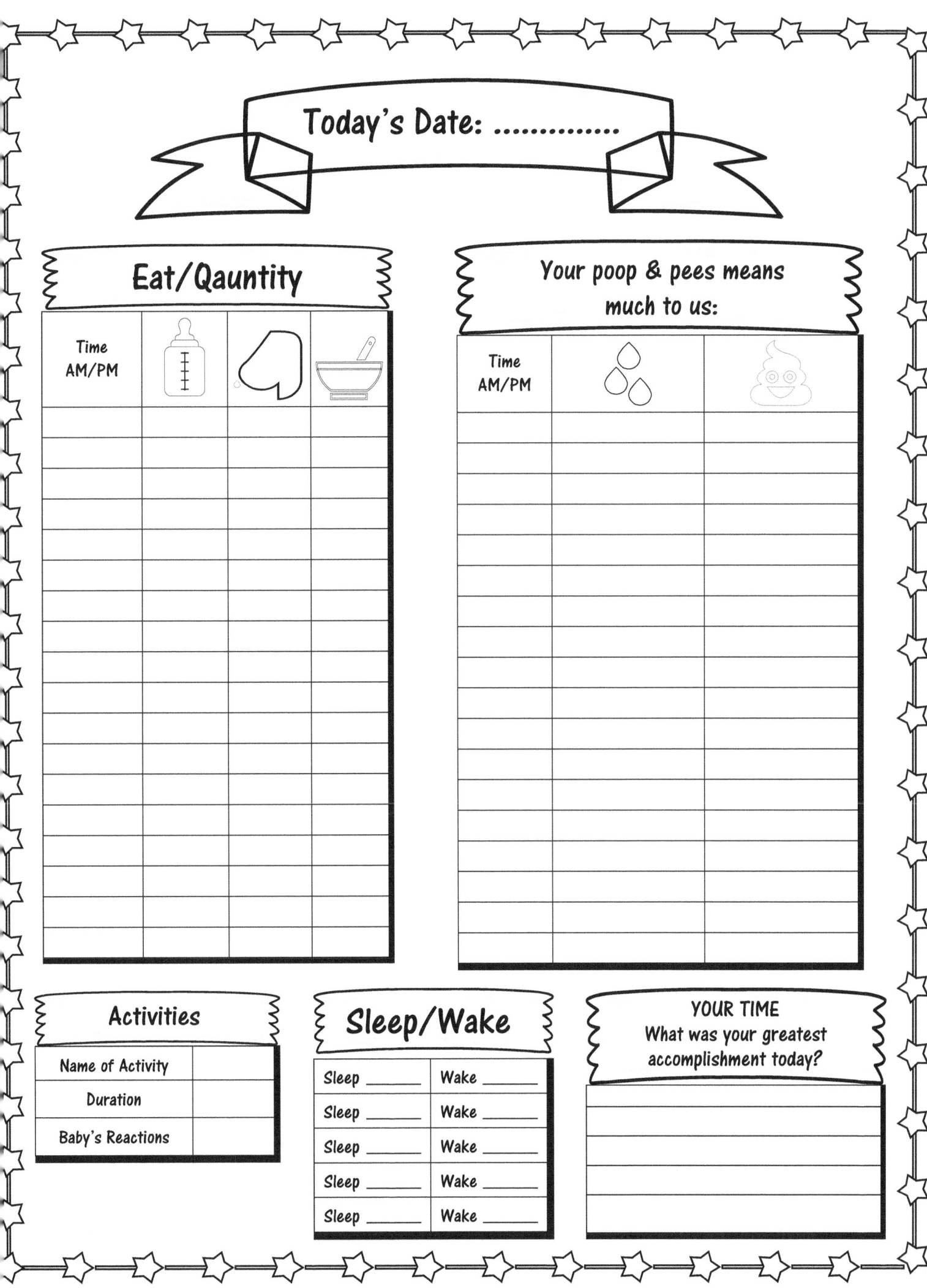

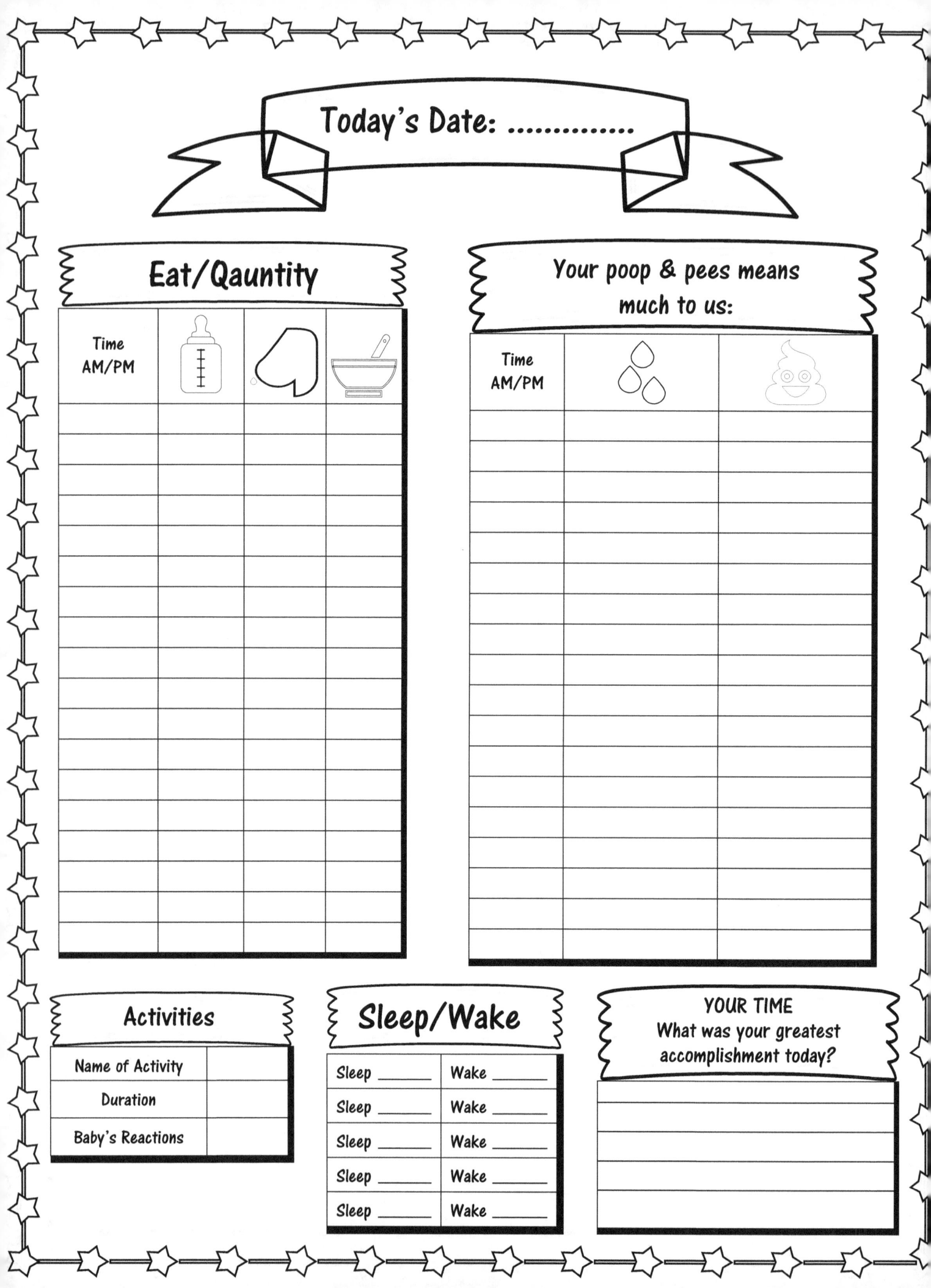

Today's Date: ....

Eat/Qauntity

Time AM/PM	🍼		🥣

Your poop & pees means much to us:

Time AM/PM	💧	💩

Activities

Name of Activity	
Duration	
Baby's Reactions	

Sleep/Wake

Sleep _____ Wake _____

Sleep _____ Wake _____

Sleep _____ Wake _____

Sleep _____ Wake _____

Sleep _____ Wake _____

YOUR TIME
What was your greatest accomplishment today?

Today's Date: ....

Eat/Qauntity

Time AM/PM	🍼	🤱	🥣

Your poop & pees means much to us:

Time AM/PM	💧	💩

Activities

Name of Activity	
Duration	
Baby's Reactions	

Sleep/Wake

Sleep _____   Wake _____
Sleep _____   Wake _____
Sleep _____   Wake _____
Sleep _____   Wake _____
Sleep _____   Wake _____

YOUR TIME
What was your greatest accomplishment today?

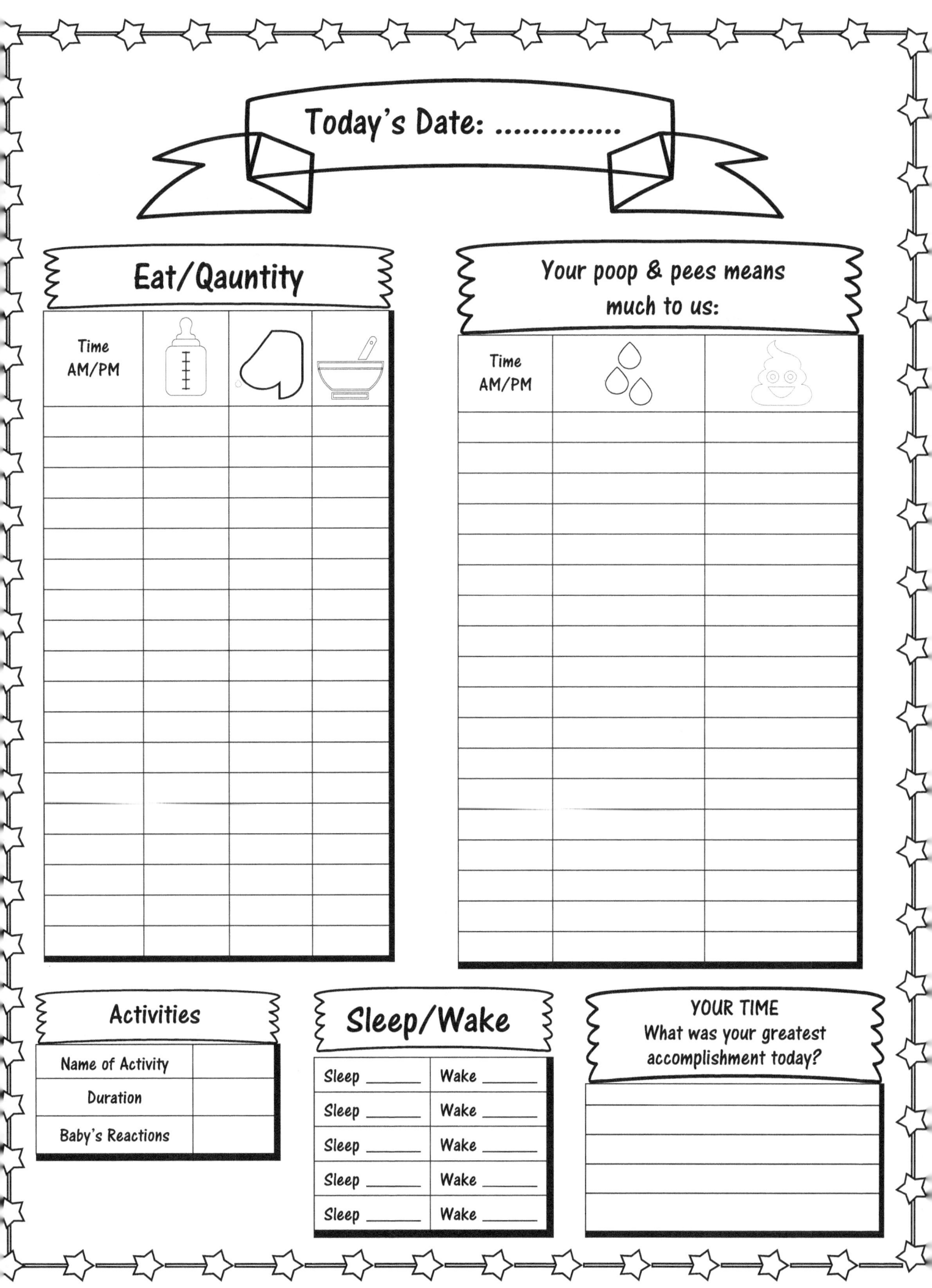

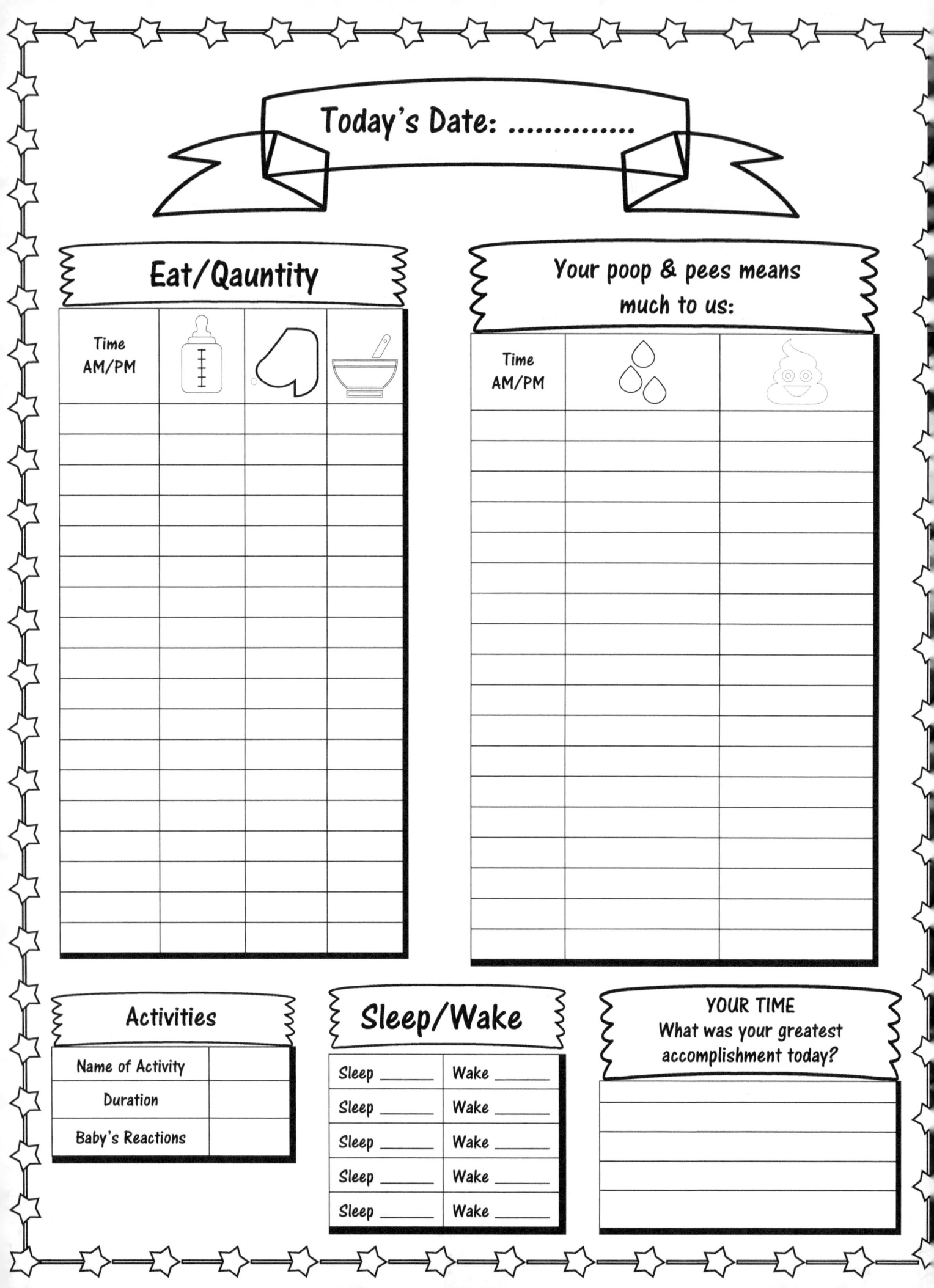

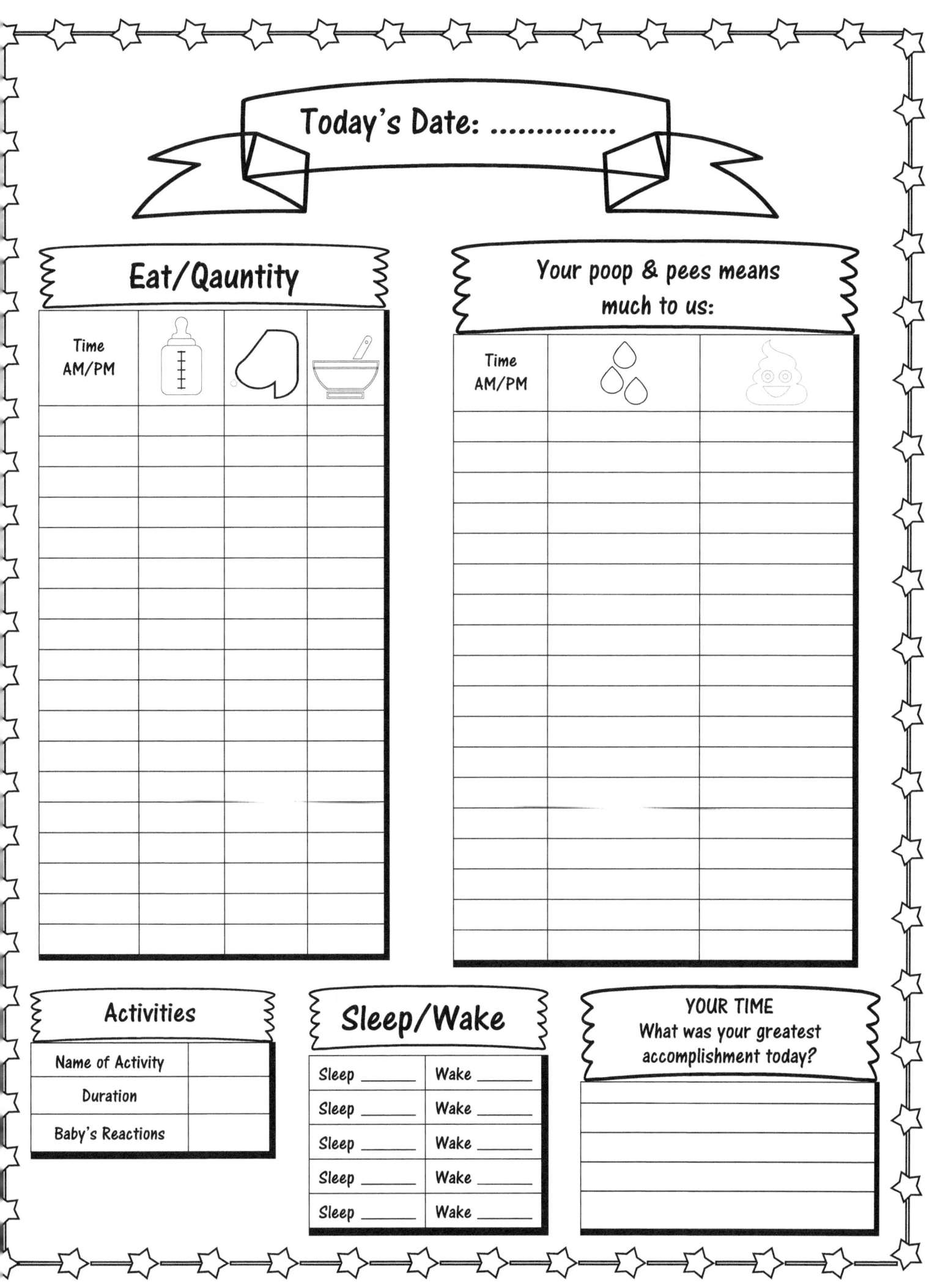

Today's Date: ....

Eat/Qauntity

Time AM/PM			

Your poop & pees means much to us:

Time AM/PM		

Activities

Name of Activity	
Duration	
Baby's Reactions	

Sleep/Wake

Sleep _____	Wake _____
Sleep _____	Wake _____
Sleep _____	Wake _____
Sleep _____	Wake _____
Sleep _____	Wake _____

YOUR TIME
What was your greatest accomplishment today?

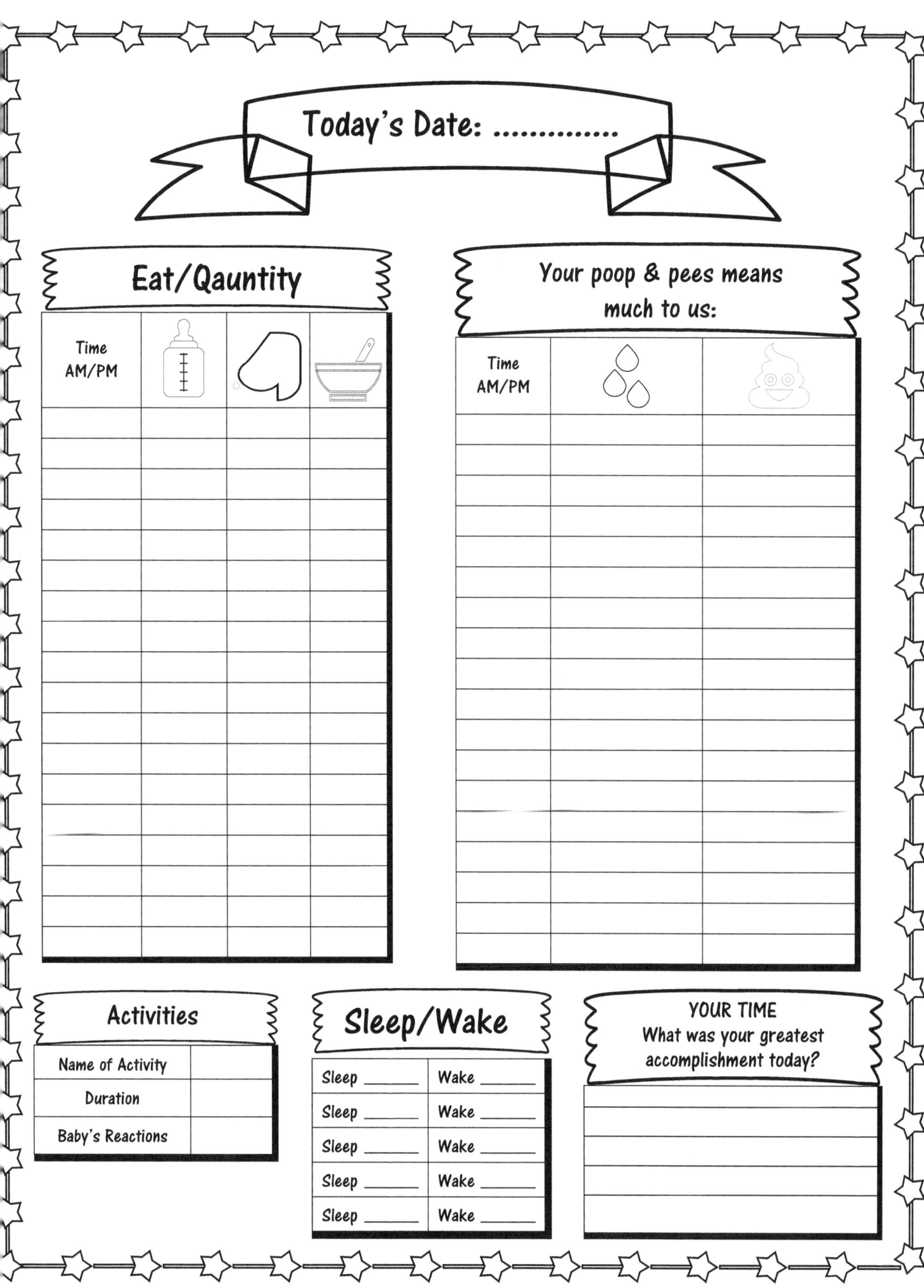

Today's Date: ....

Eat/Qauntity

Time AM/PM	🍼	🤱	🥣

Your poop & pees means much to us:

Time AM/PM	💧	💩

Activities

Name of Activity	
Duration	
Baby's Reactions	

Sleep/Wake

Sleep _____ Wake _____
Sleep _____ Wake _____
Sleep _____ Wake _____
Sleep _____ Wake _____
Sleep _____ Wake _____

YOUR TIME
What was your greatest accomplishment today?

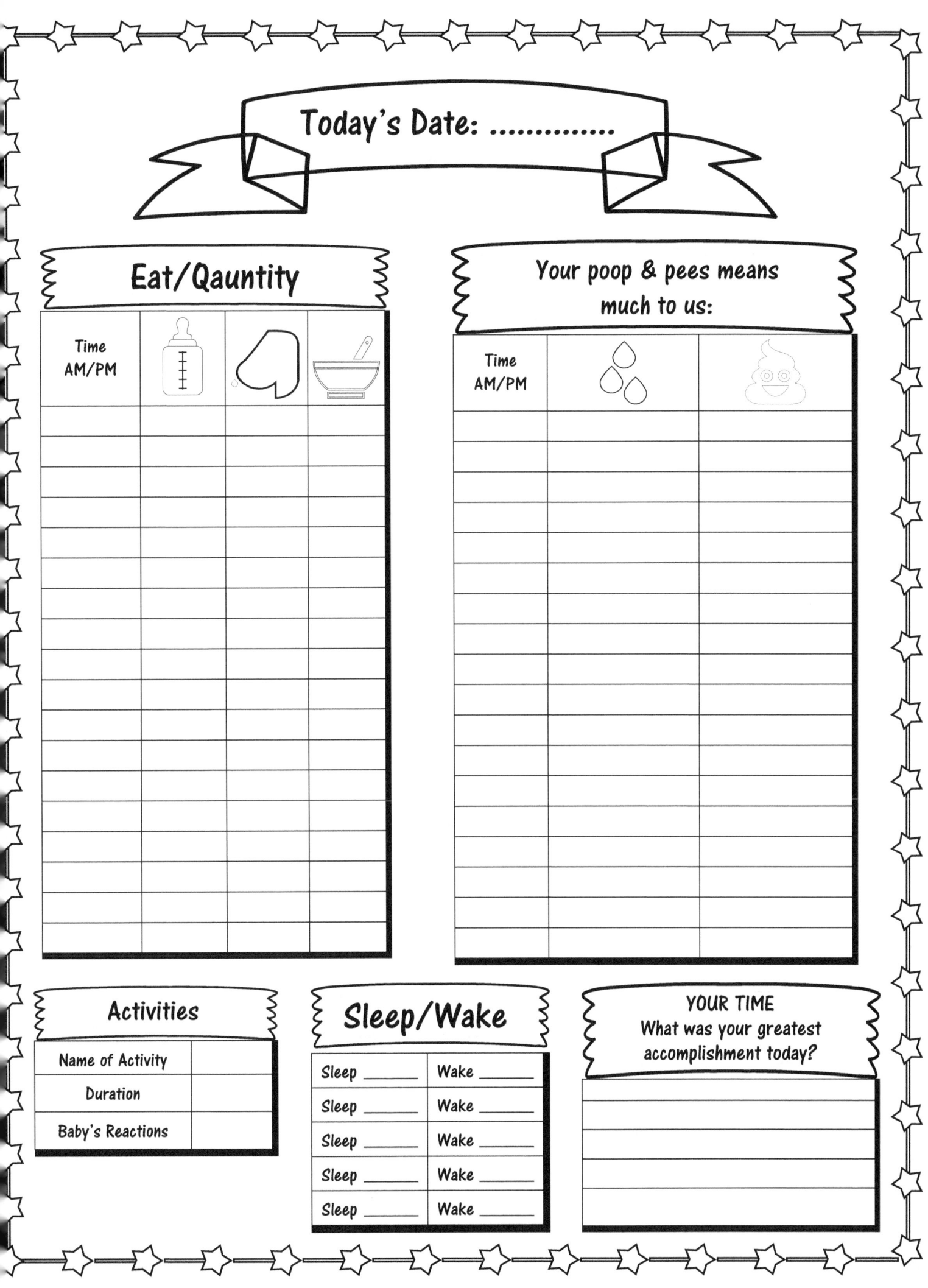

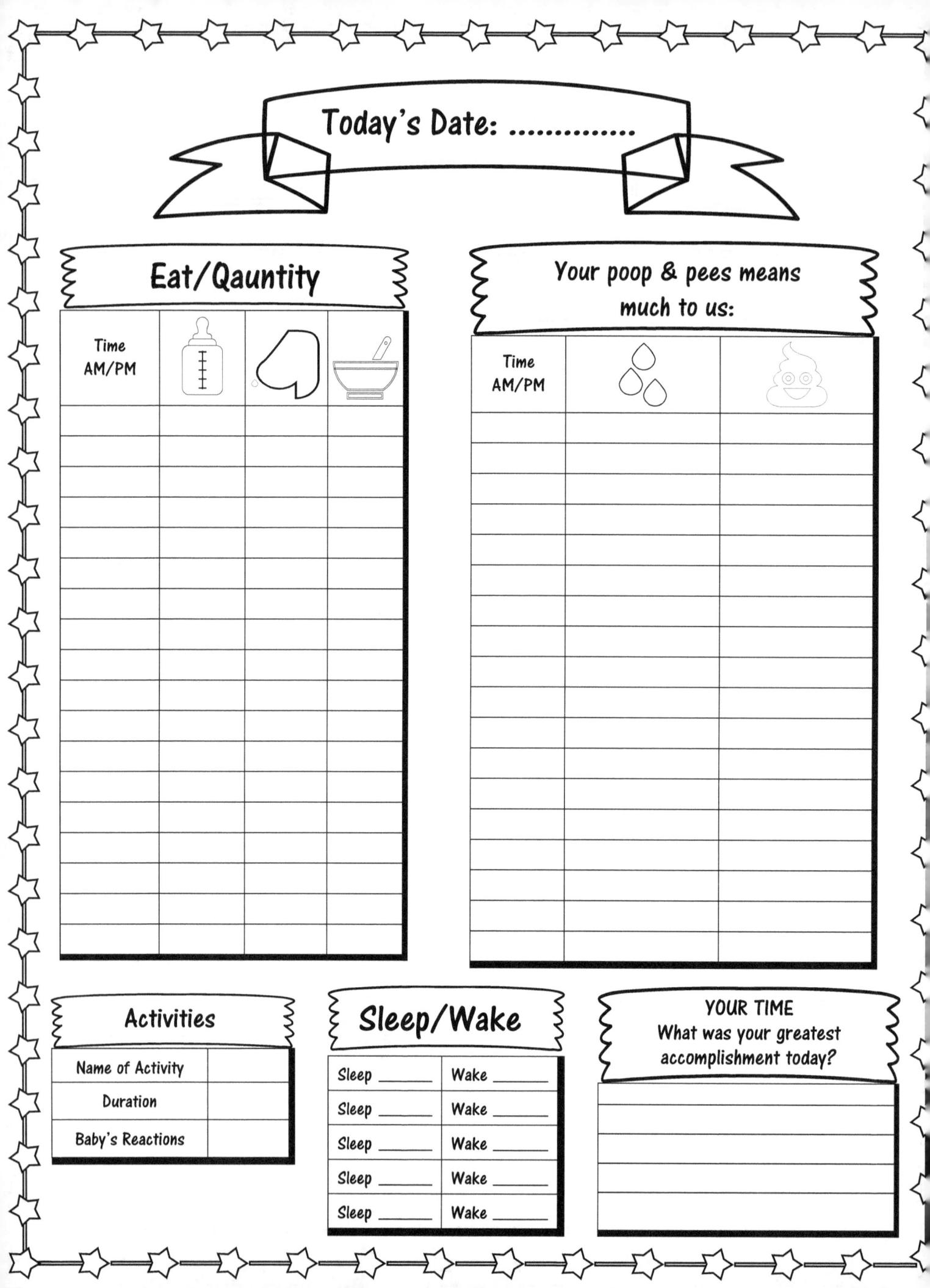

Today's Date: ....

Eat/Qauntity

Time AM/PM	🍼	🤱	🥣

Your poop & pees means much to us:

Time AM/PM	💧	💩

Activities

Name of Activity	
Duration	
Baby's Reactions	

Sleep/Wake

Sleep _____   Wake _____

Sleep _____   Wake _____

Sleep _____   Wake _____

Sleep _____   Wake _____

Sleep _____   Wake _____

YOUR TIME
What was your greatest accomplishment today?

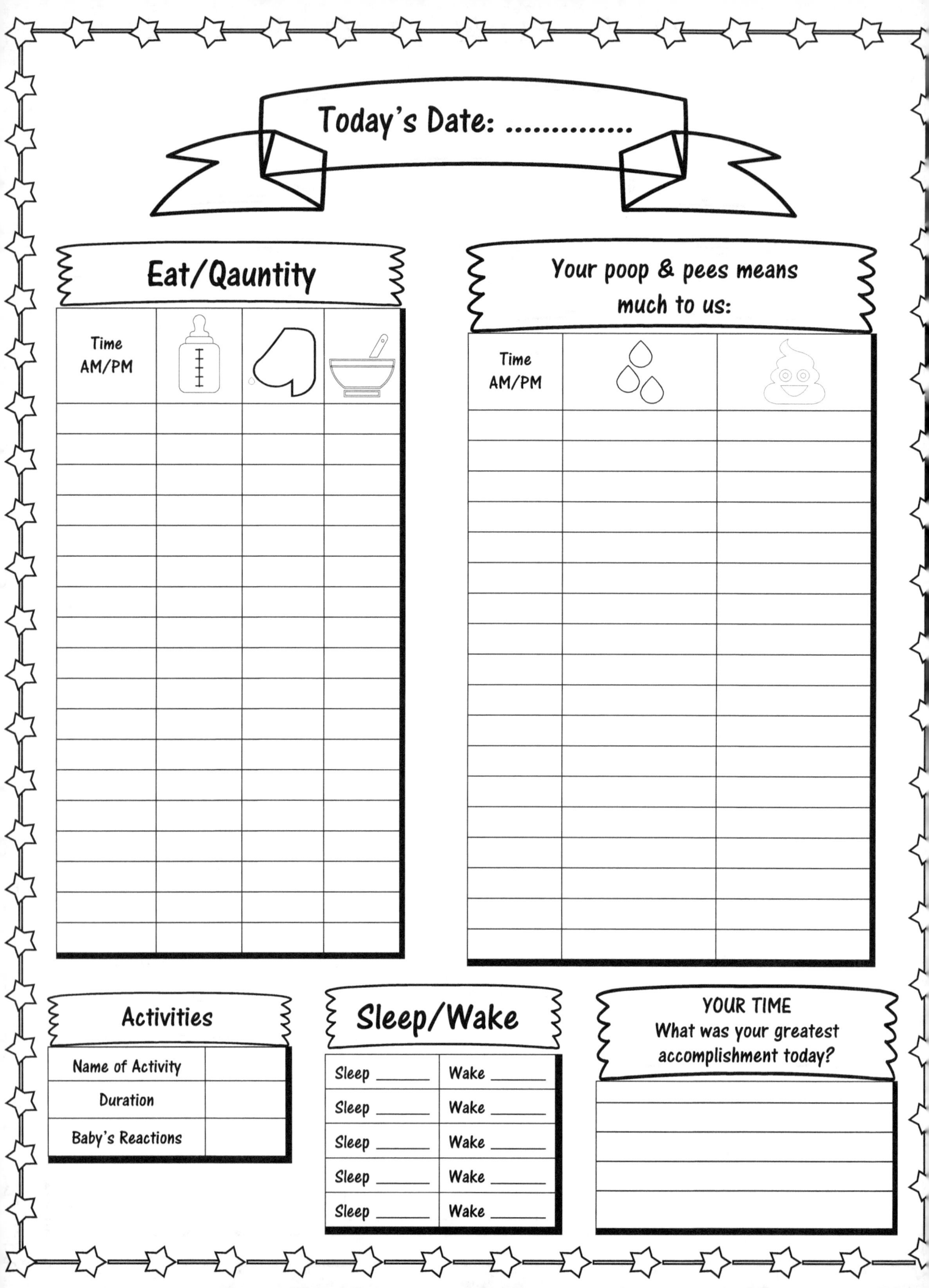

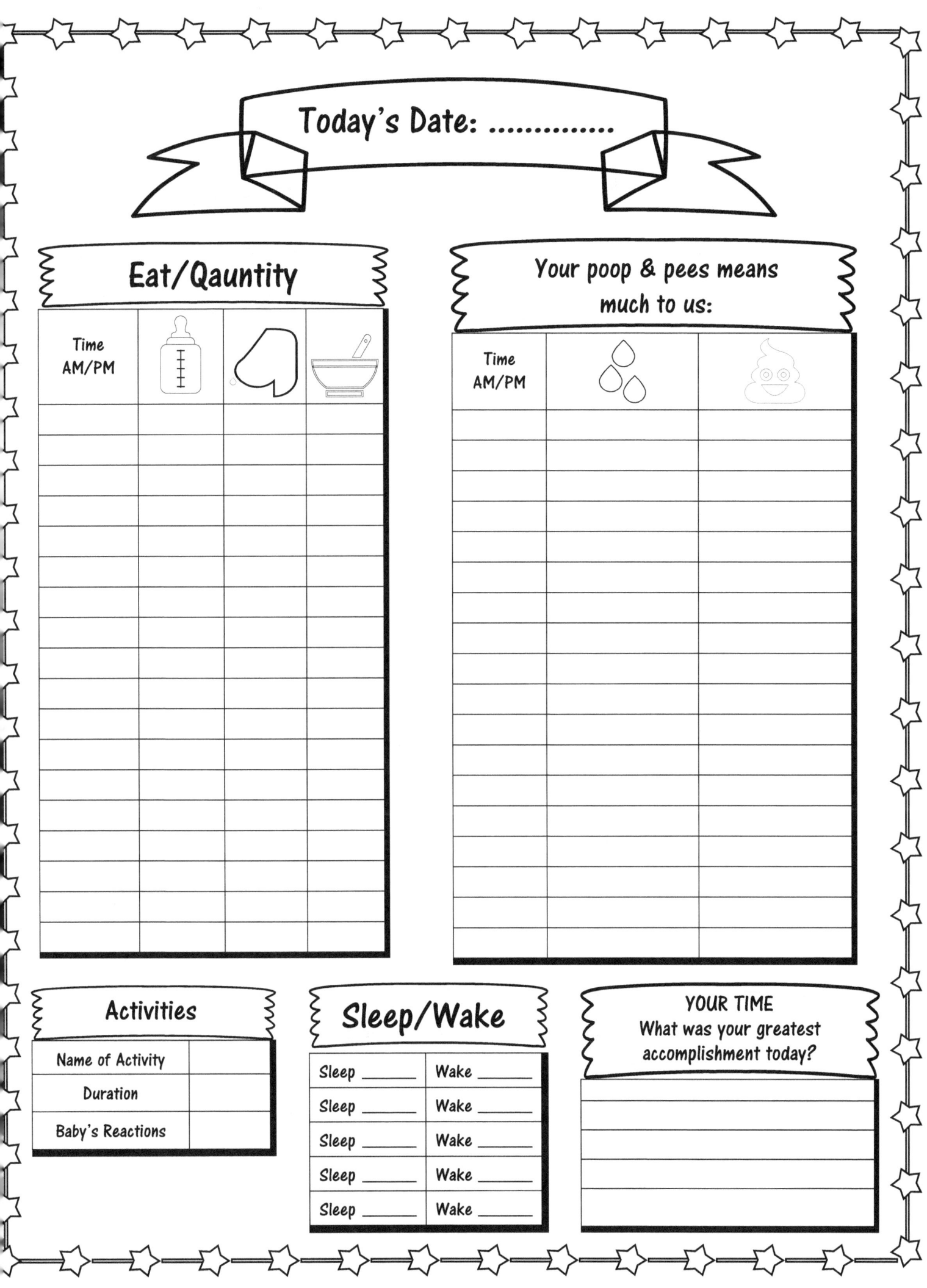

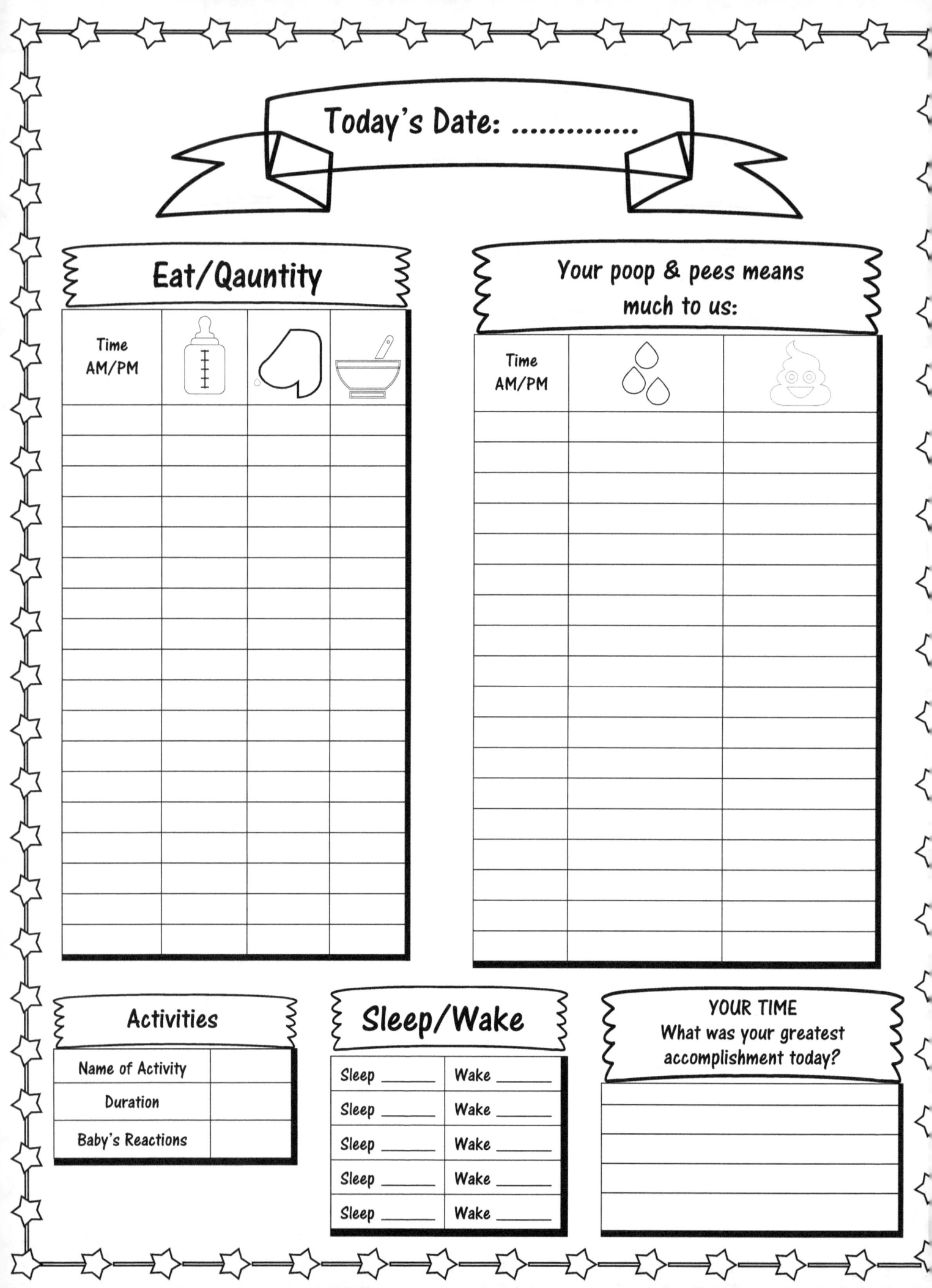

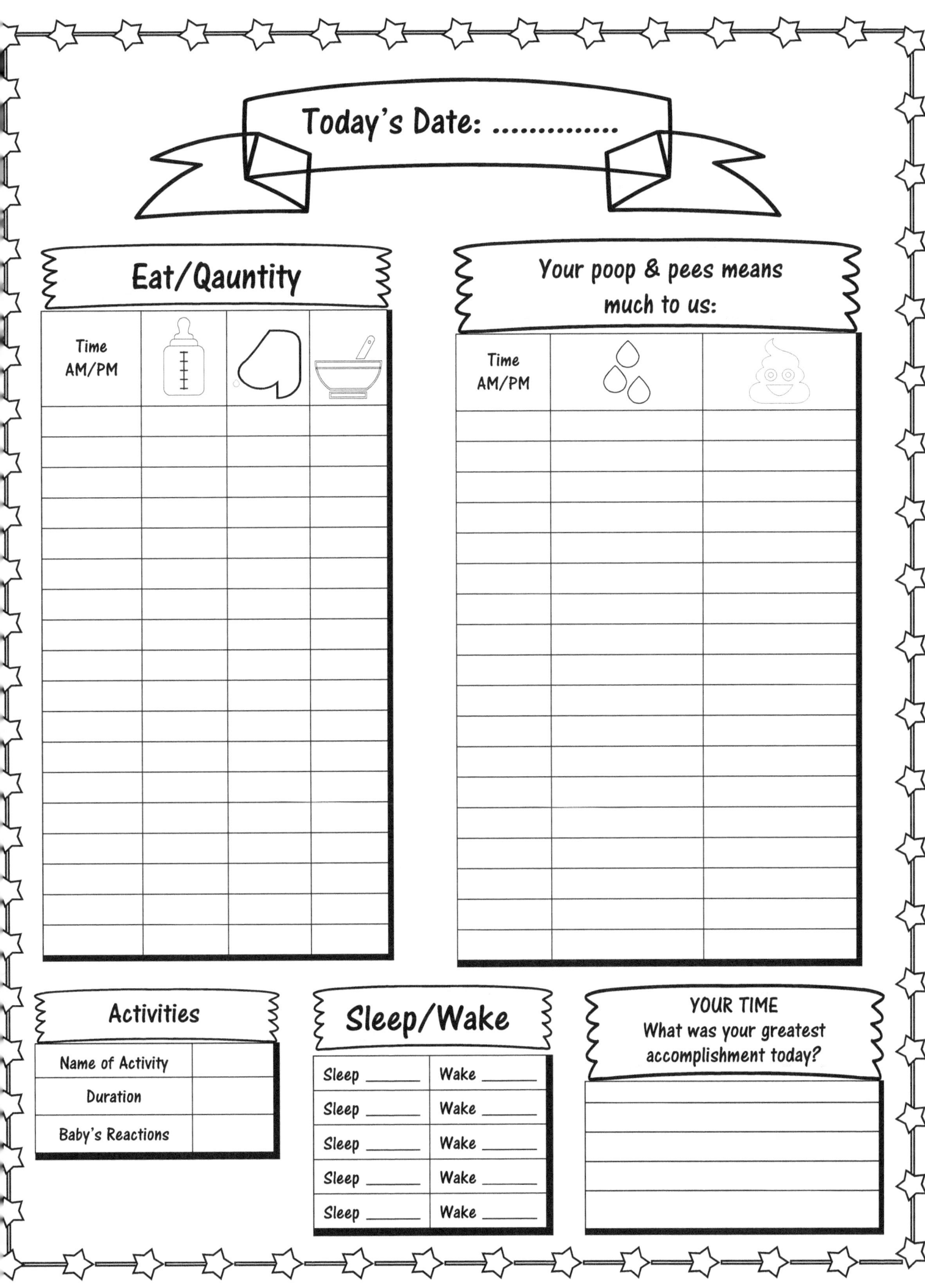

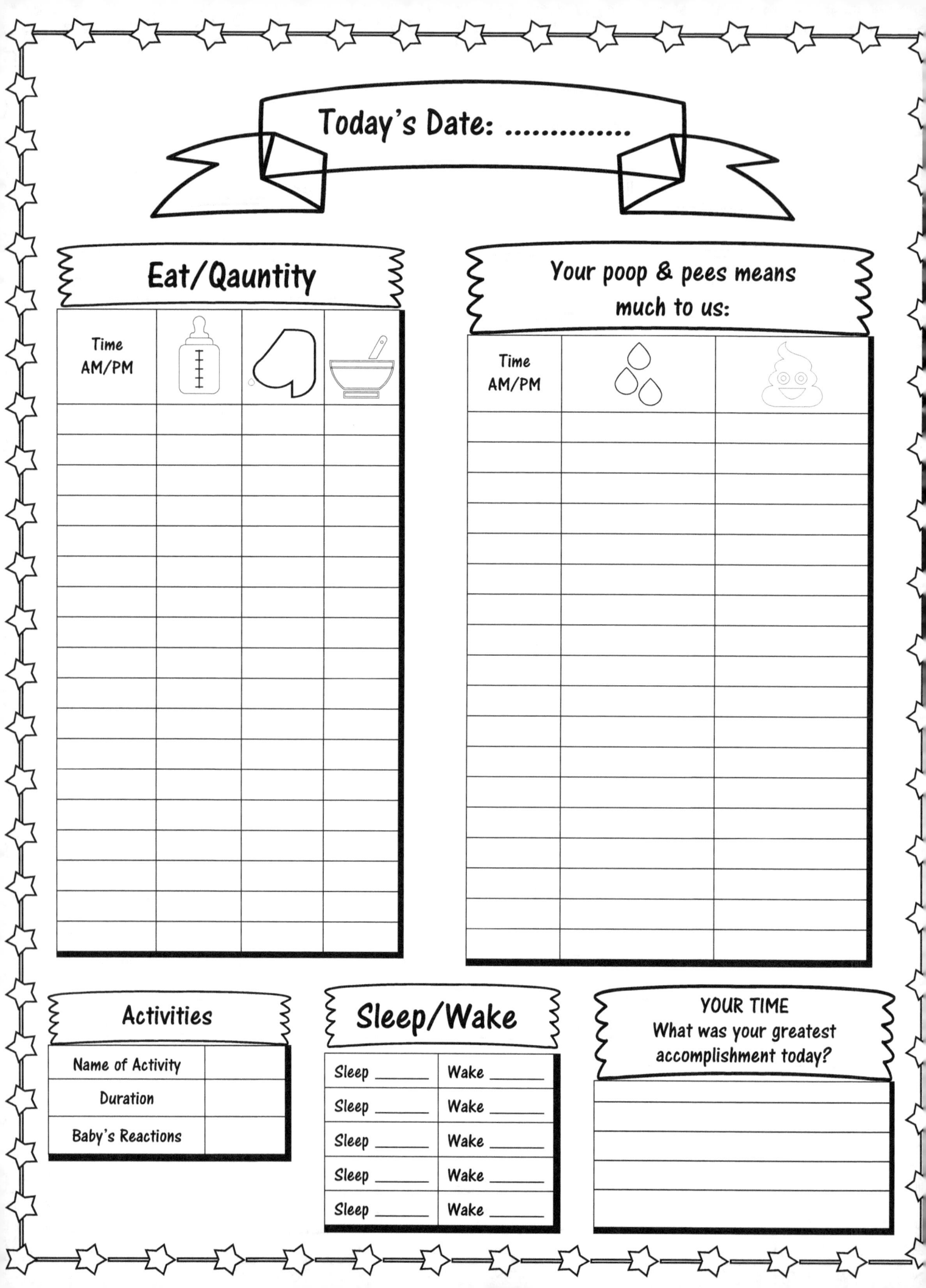

Today's Date: ....

Eat/Qauntity

Time AM/PM	🍼	🤱	🥣

Your poop & pees means much to us:

Time AM/PM	💧	💩

Activities

Name of Activity	
Duration	
Baby's Reactions	

Sleep/Wake

Sleep _____ Wake _____
Sleep _____ Wake _____
Sleep _____ Wake _____
Sleep _____ Wake _____
Sleep _____ Wake _____

YOUR TIME
What was your greatest accomplishment today?

Today's Date: ....

Eat/Qauntity

Time AM/PM	🍼	🤱	🥣

Your poop & pees means much to us:

Time AM/PM	💧	💩

Activities

Name of Activity	
Duration	
Baby's Reactions	

Sleep/Wake

Sleep _____ Wake _____
Sleep _____ Wake _____
Sleep _____ Wake _____
Sleep _____ Wake _____
Sleep _____ Wake _____

YOUR TIME
What was your greatest accomplishment today?

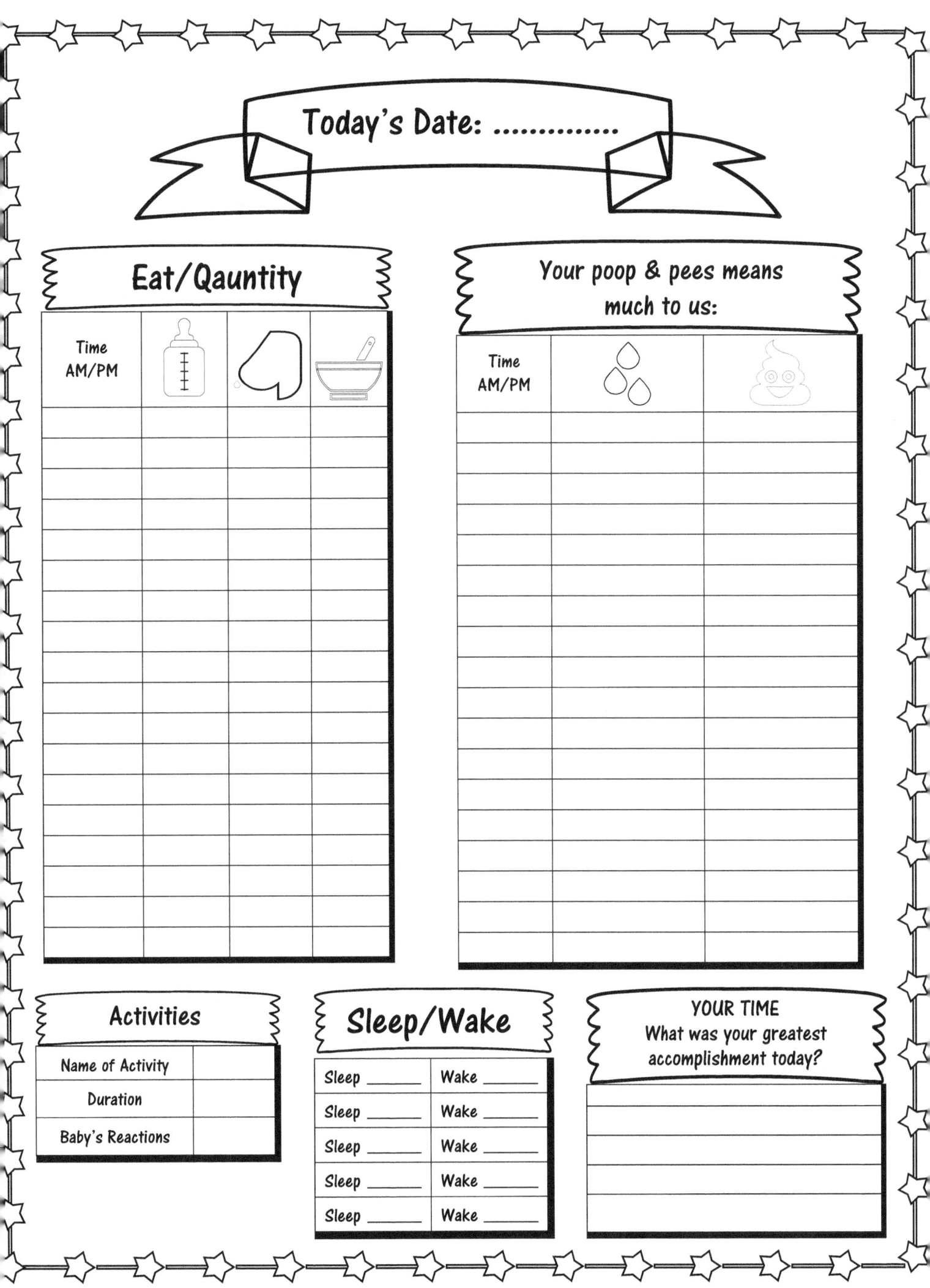

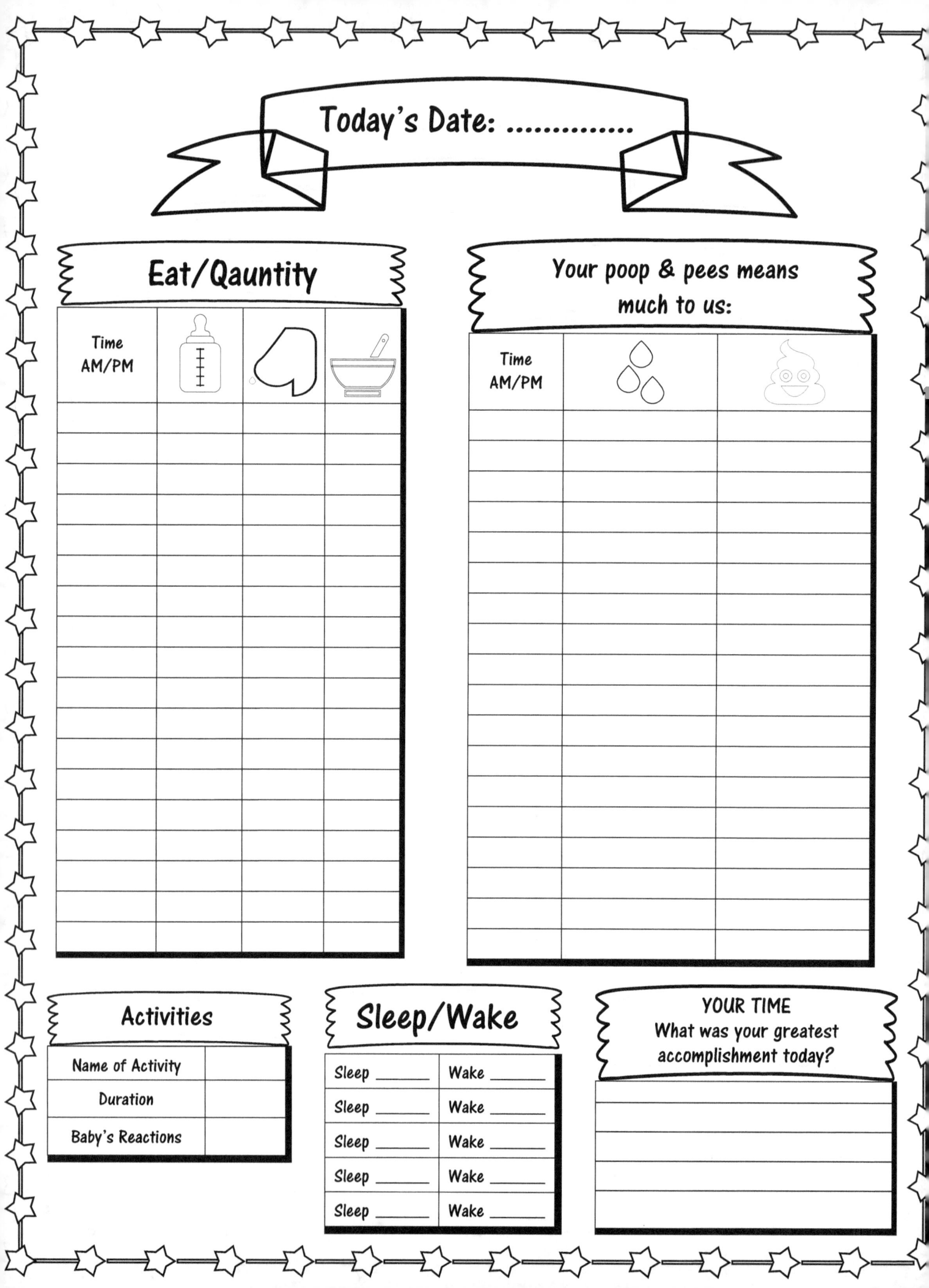

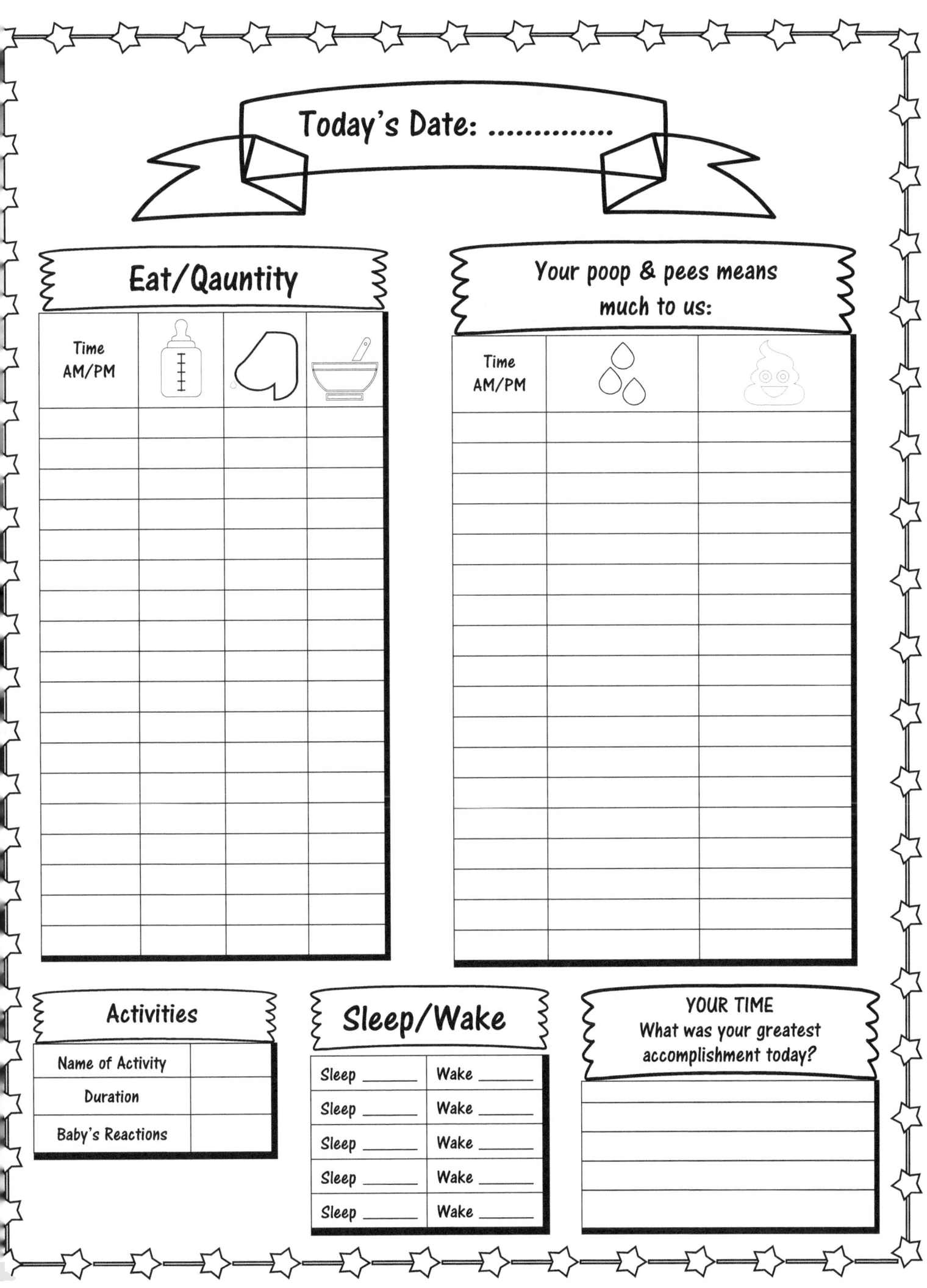

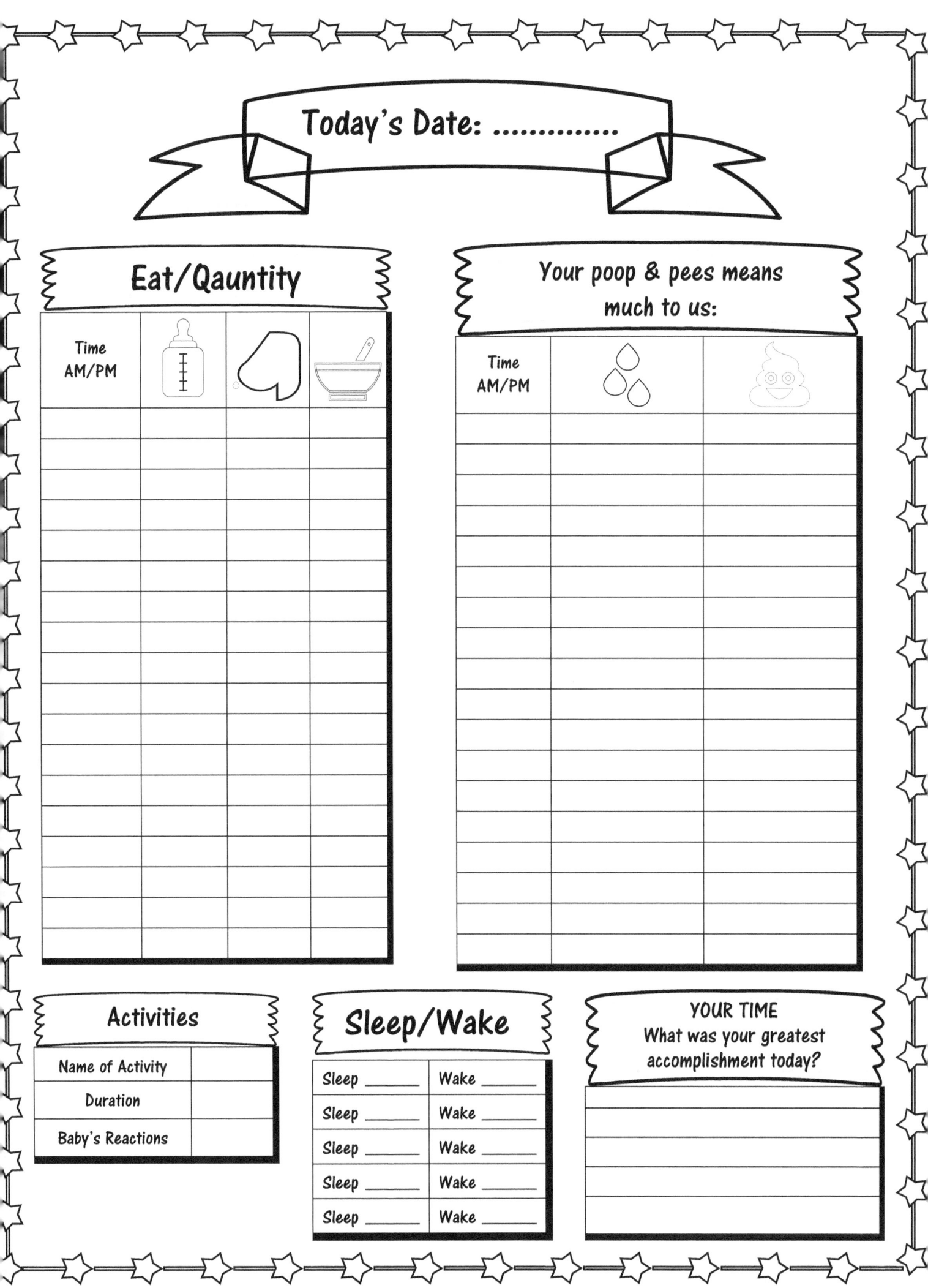

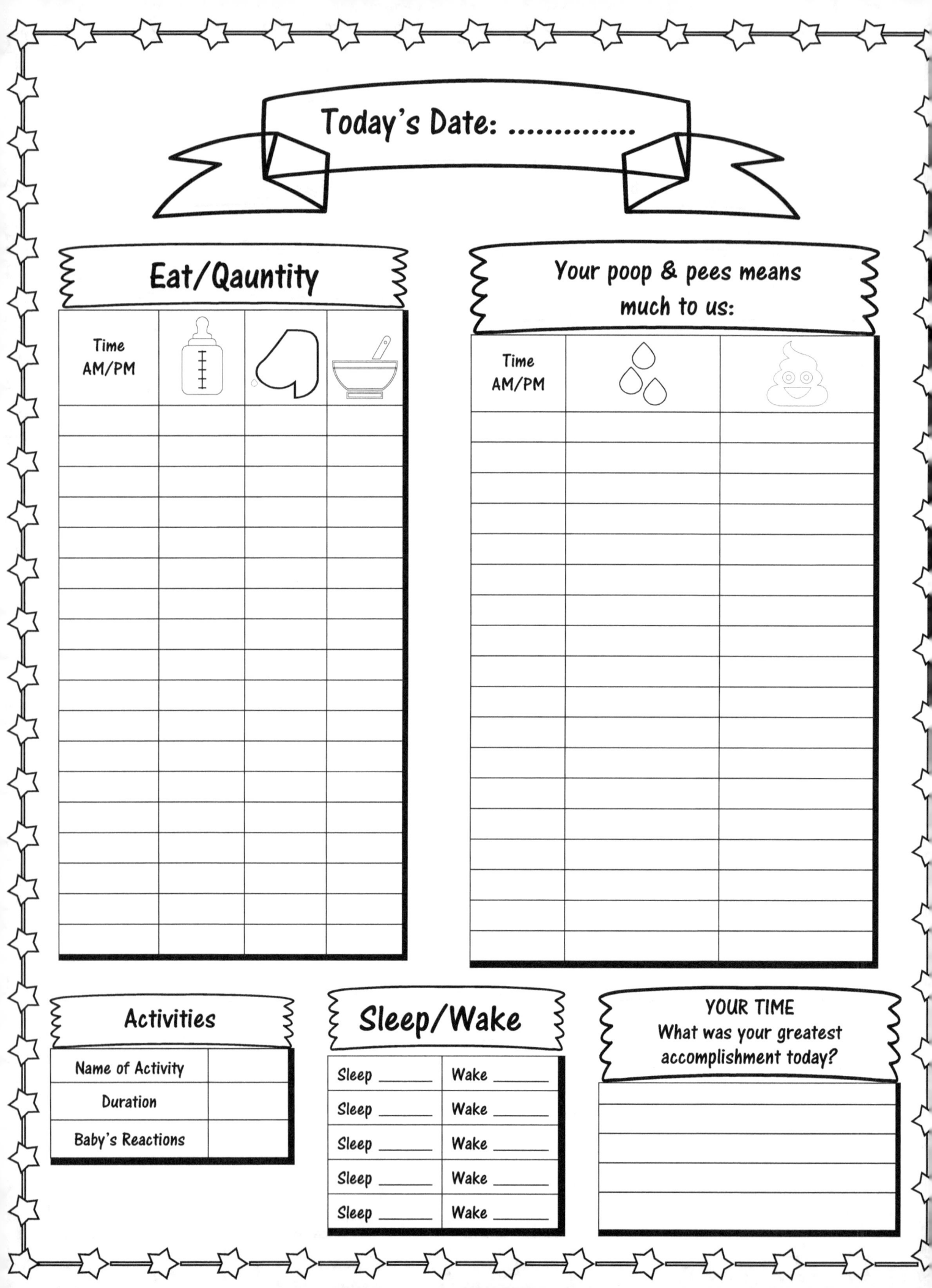

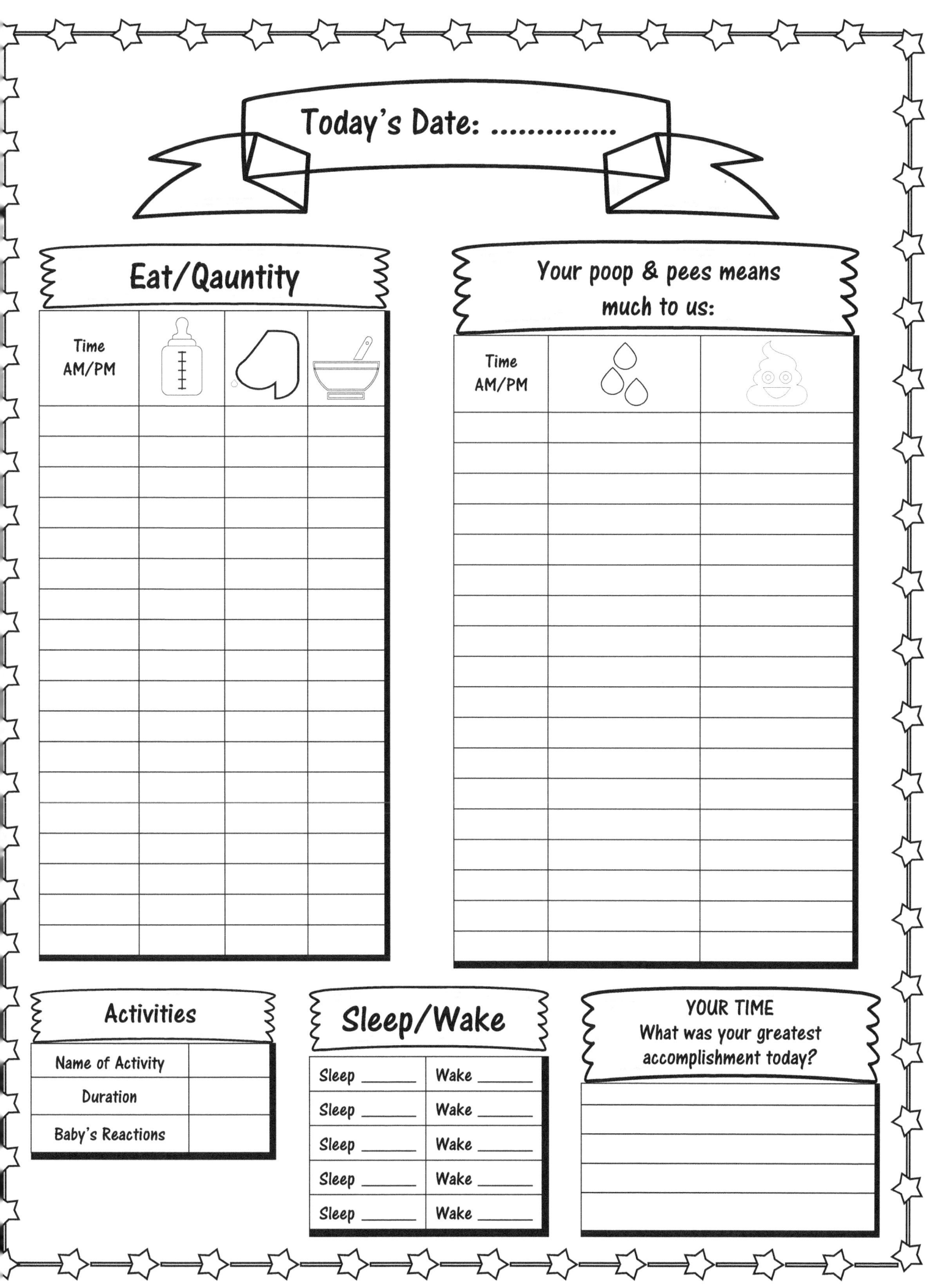

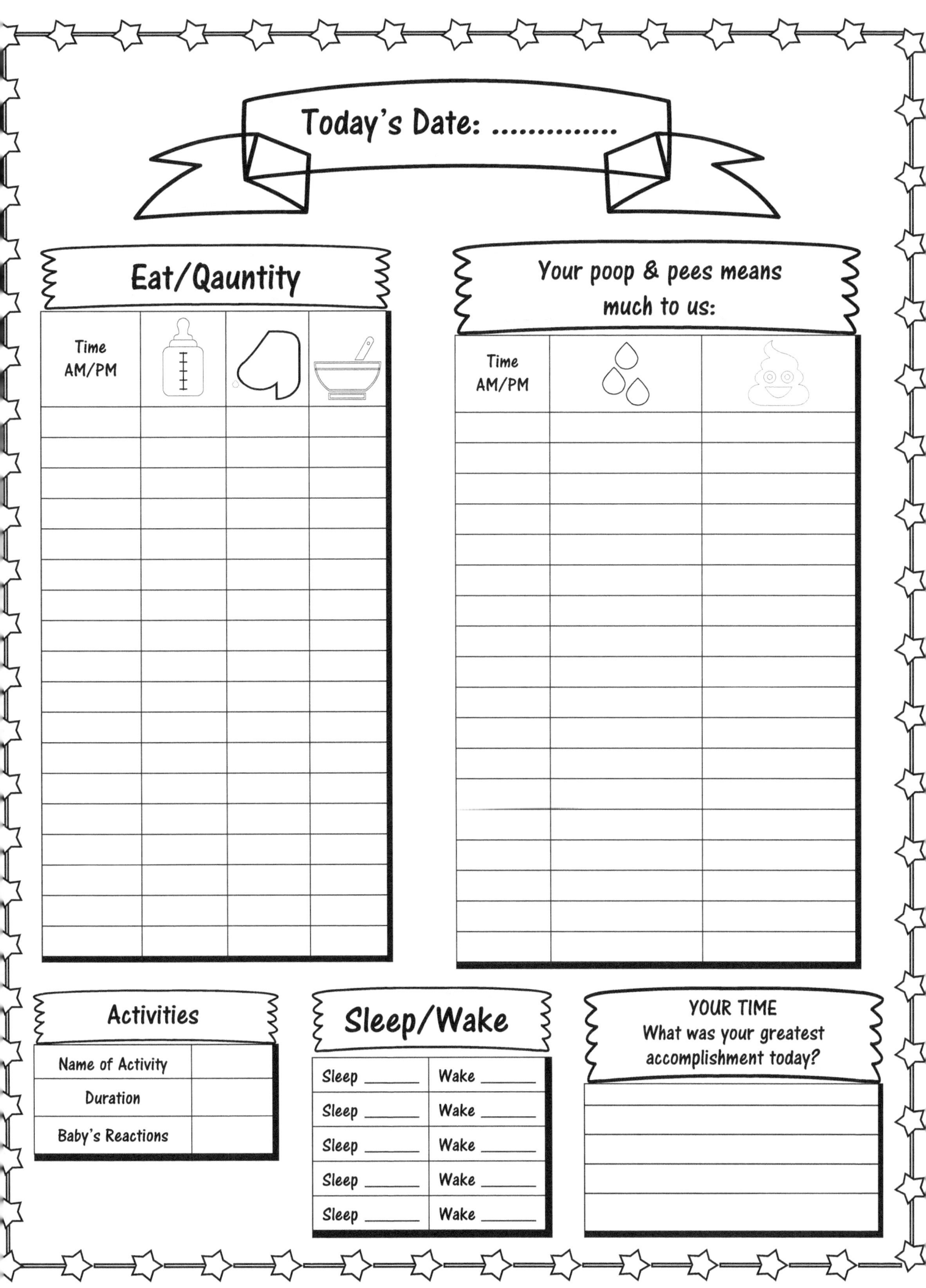

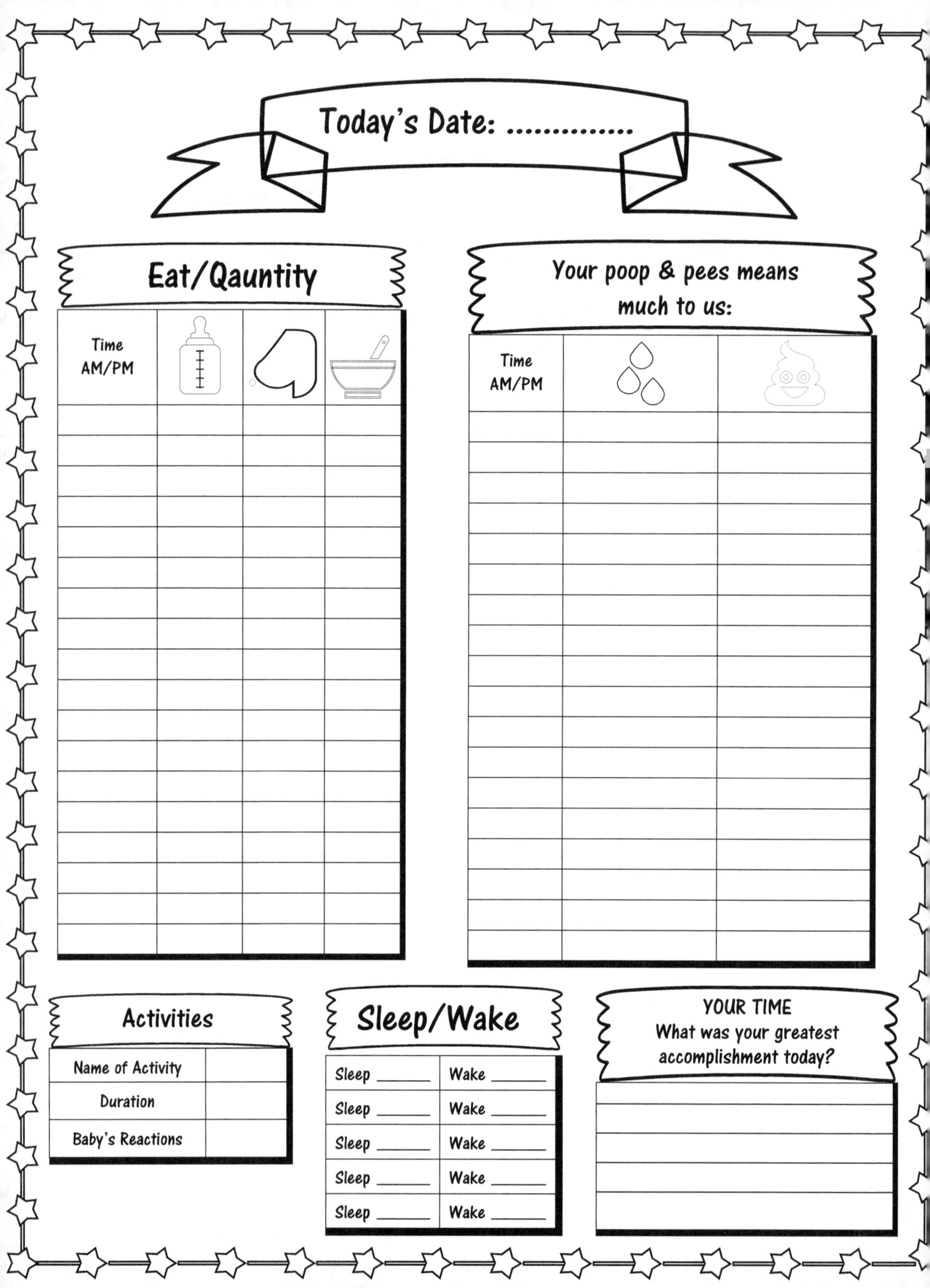

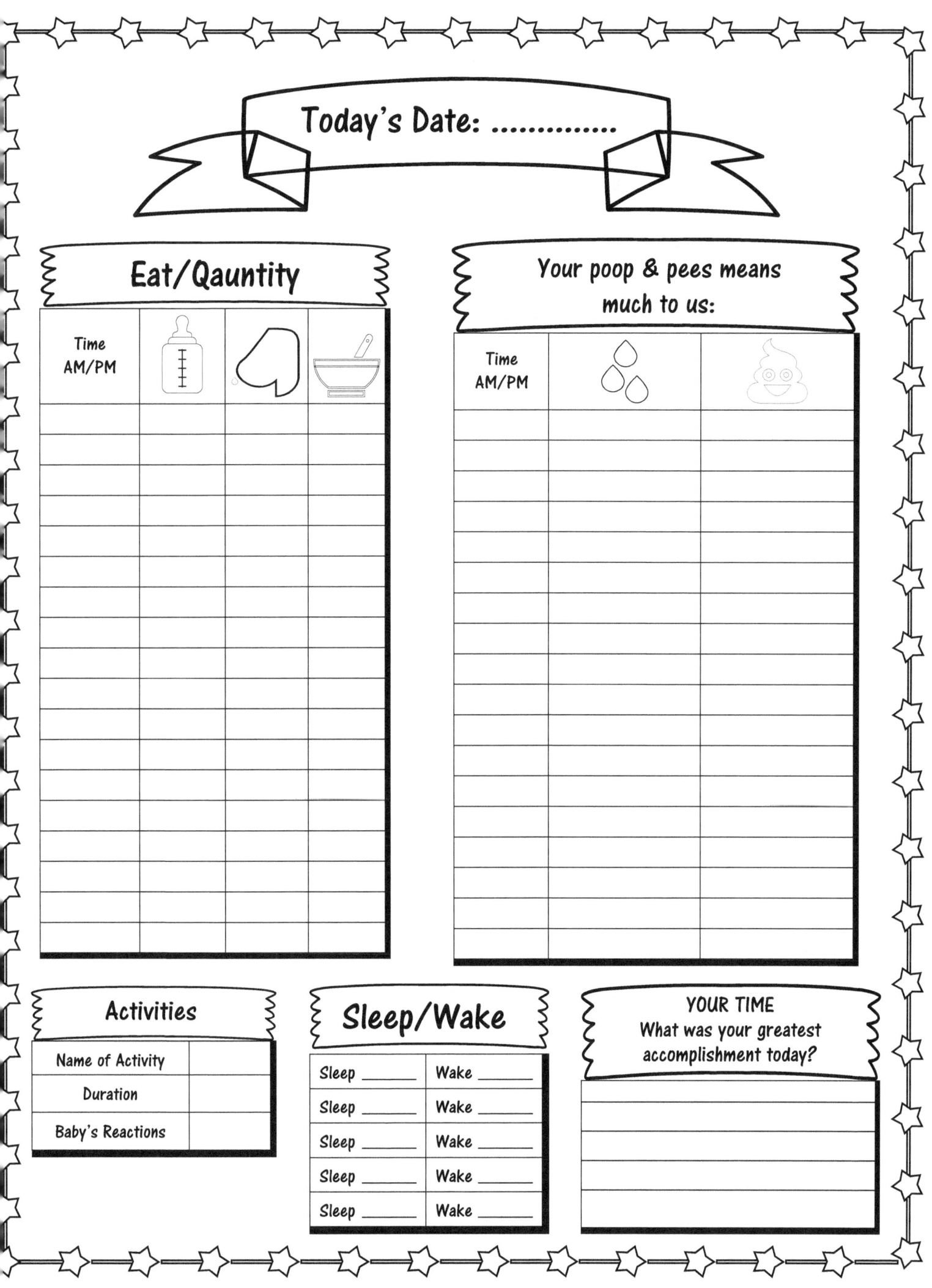

Today's Date: ....

Eat/Qauntity

Time AM/PM	🍼	🤱	🥣

Your poop & pees means much to us:

Time AM/PM	💧	💩

Activities

Name of Activity	
Duration	
Baby's Reactions	

Sleep/Wake

Sleep _____   Wake _____
Sleep _____   Wake _____
Sleep _____   Wake _____
Sleep _____   Wake _____
Sleep _____   Wake _____

YOUR TIME
What was your greatest accomplishment today?

Today's Date: ....

Eat/Qauntity

Time AM/PM	🍼	🥛	🥣

Your poop & pees means much to us:

Time AM/PM	💧	💩

Activities

Name of Activity	
Duration	
Baby's Reactions	

Sleep/Wake

Sleep _____   Wake _____

Sleep _____   Wake _____

Sleep _____   Wake _____

Sleep _____   Wake _____

Sleep _____   Wake _____

YOUR TIME
What was your greatest accomplishment today?

Today's Date: ....

Eat/Qauntity

Time AM/PM	🍼		🥣

Your poop & pees means much to us:

Time AM/PM	💧	💩

Activities

Name of Activity	
Duration	
Baby's Reactions	

Sleep/Wake

Sleep _____ Wake _____

Sleep _____ Wake _____

Sleep _____ Wake _____

Sleep _____ Wake _____

Sleep _____ Wake _____

YOUR TIME
What was your greatest accomplishment today?

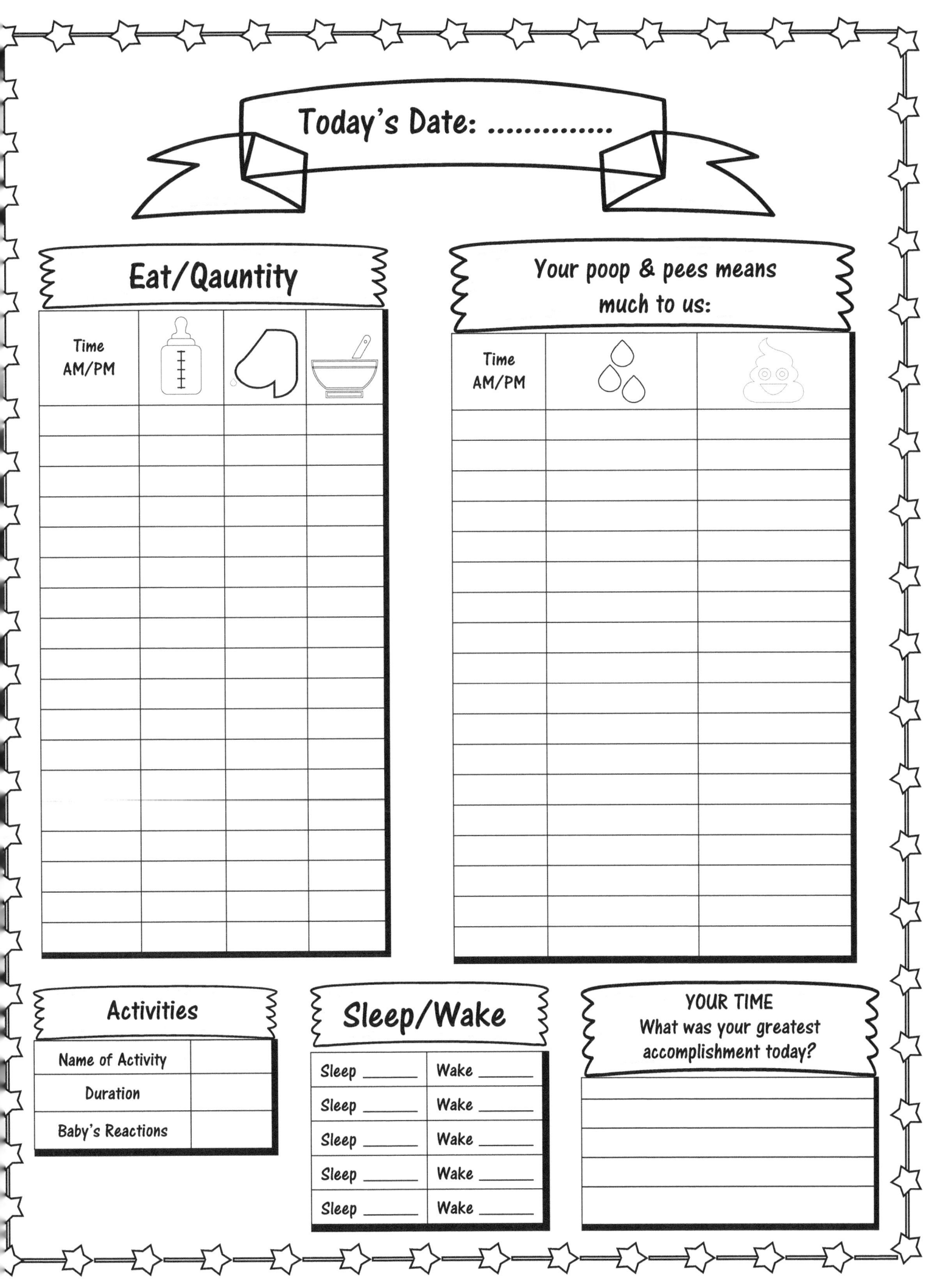

Today's Date: ....

Eat/Qauntity

Time AM/PM	🍼	🤱	🥣

Your poop & pees means much to us:

Time AM/PM	💧	💩

Activities

Name of Activity	
Duration	
Baby's Reactions	

Sleep/Wake

Sleep _____ Wake _____
Sleep _____ Wake _____
Sleep _____ Wake _____
Sleep _____ Wake _____
Sleep _____ Wake _____

YOUR TIME
What was your greatest accomplishment today?

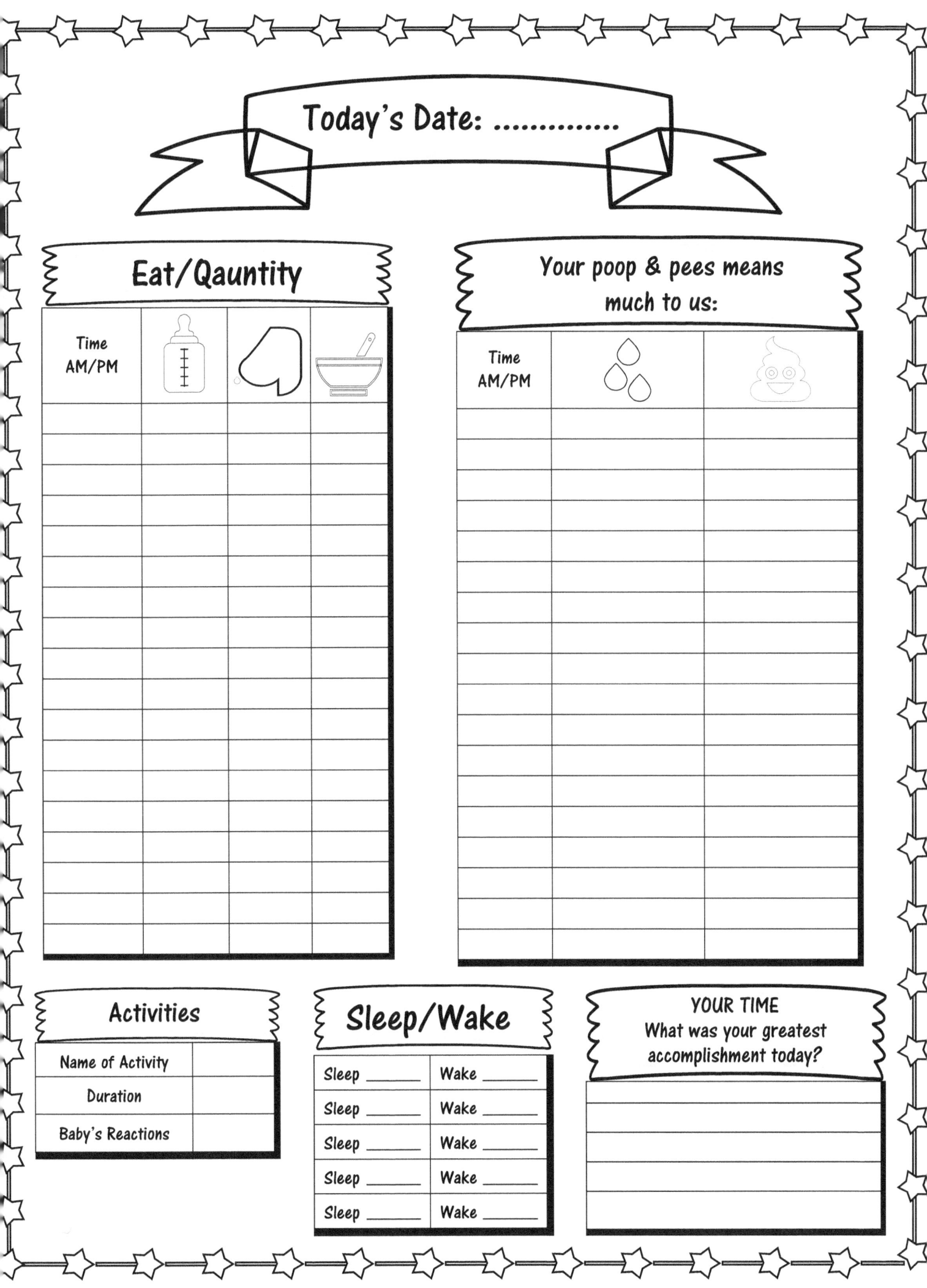

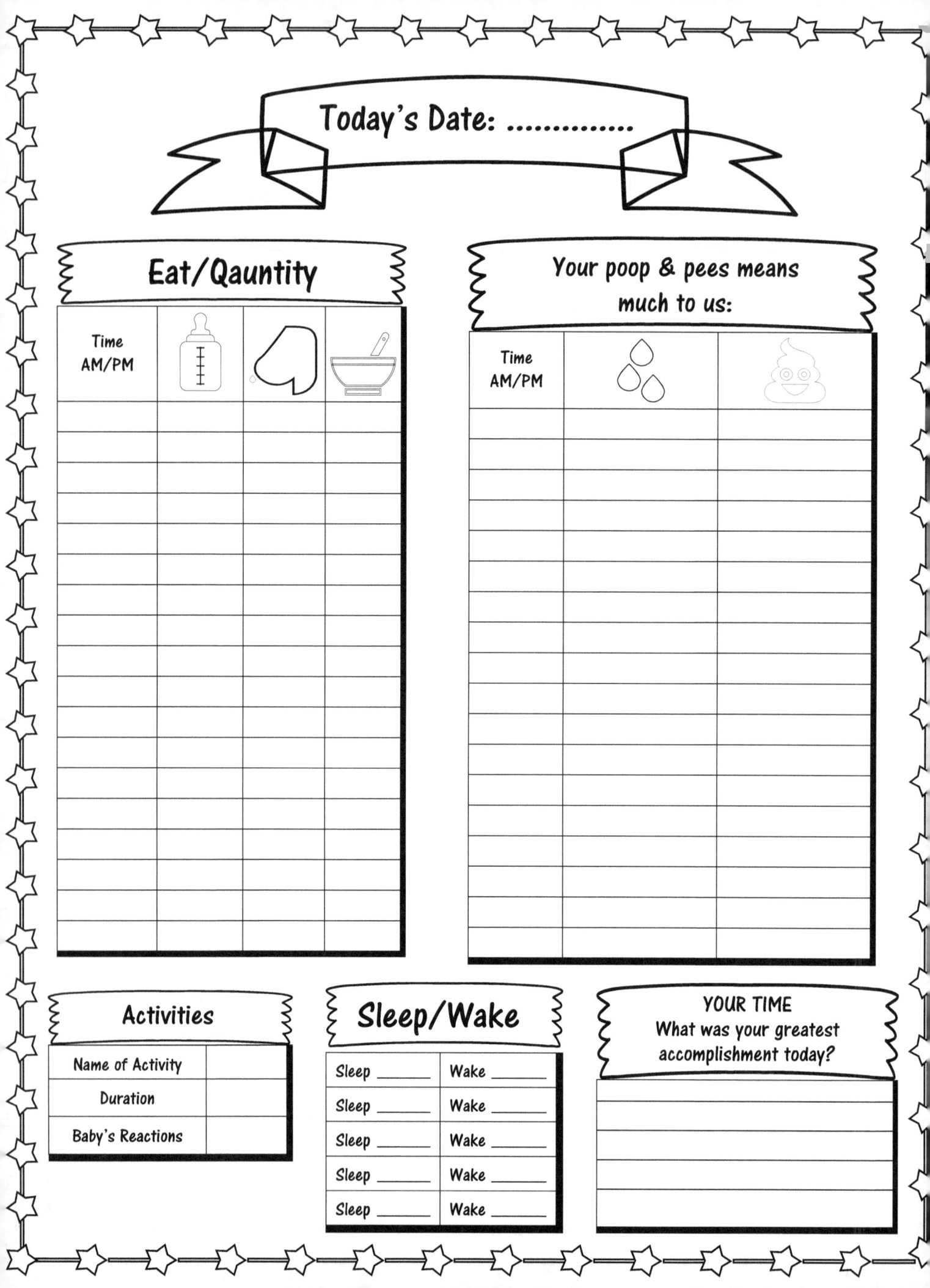

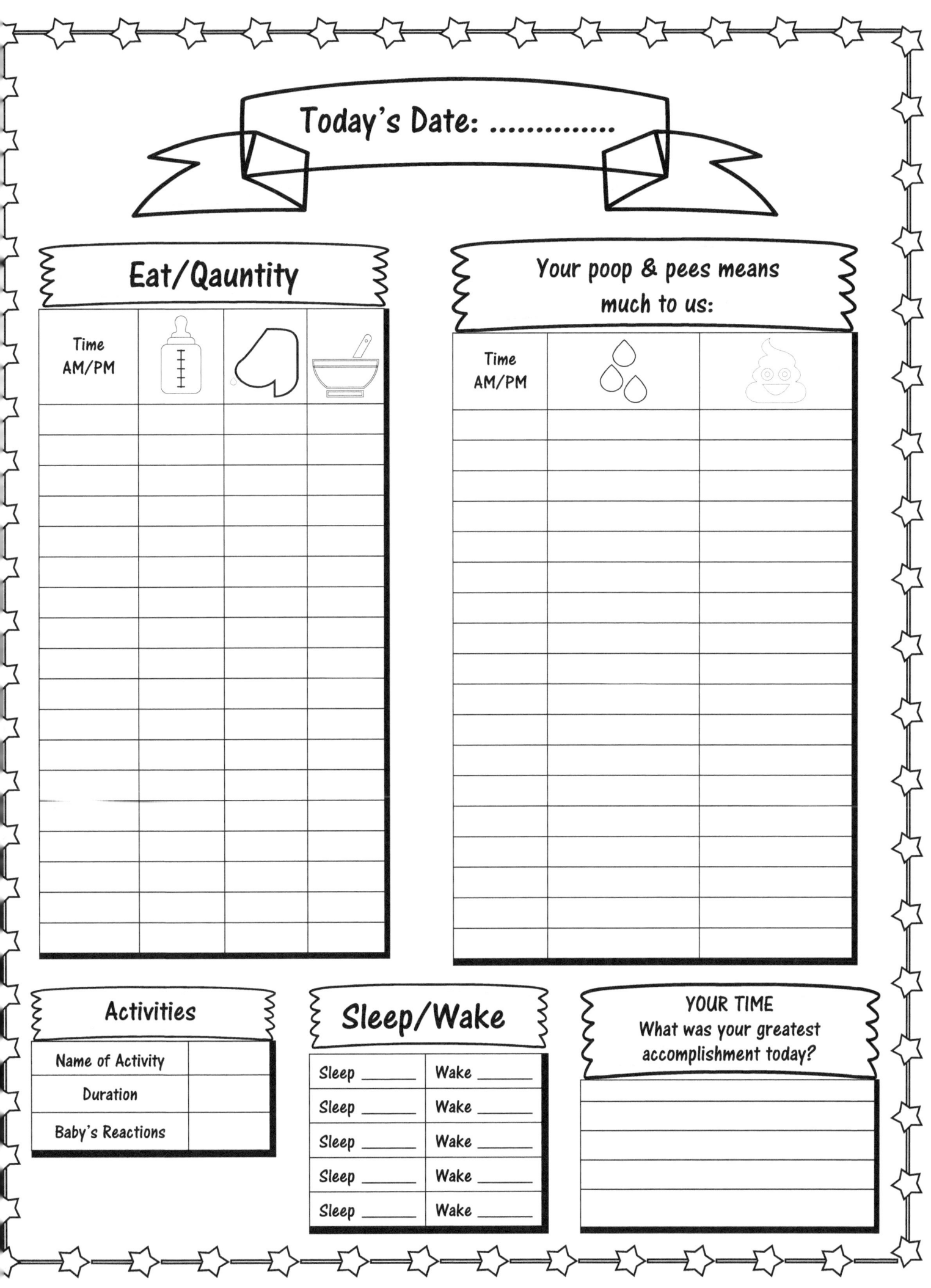

Today's Date: ....

Eat/Qauntity

Time AM/PM	🍼		🥣

Your poop & pees means much to us:

Time AM/PM	💧	💩

Activities

Name of Activity	
Duration	
Baby's Reactions	

Sleep/Wake

Sleep _____ Wake _____
Sleep _____ Wake _____
Sleep _____ Wake _____
Sleep _____ Wake _____
Sleep _____ Wake _____

YOUR TIME
What was your greatest accomplishment today?

Today's Date: ....

Eat/Qauntity

Time AM/PM	🍼		🥣

Your poop & pees means much to us:

Time AM/PM	💧	💩

Activities

Name of Activity	
Duration	
Baby's Reactions	

Sleep/Wake

Sleep _____ Wake _____
Sleep _____ Wake _____
Sleep _____ Wake _____
Sleep _____ Wake _____
Sleep _____ Wake _____

YOUR TIME
What was your greatest accomplishment today?

Today's Date: ....

Eat/Qauntity

Time AM/PM	🍼		🥣

Your poop & pees means much to us:

Time AM/PM	💧	💩

Activities

Name of Activity	
Duration	
Baby's Reactions	

Sleep/Wake

Sleep _____ Wake _____
Sleep _____ Wake _____
Sleep _____ Wake _____
Sleep _____ Wake _____
Sleep _____ Wake _____

YOUR TIME
What was your greatest accomplishment today?

_____
_____
_____
_____
_____

Today's Date: ....

Eat/Qauntity

Time AM/PM	🍼	🤱	🥣

Your poop & pees means much to us:

Time AM/PM	💧💧	💩

Activities

Name of Activity	
Duration	
Baby's Reactions	

Sleep/Wake

Sleep _____ Wake _____
Sleep _____ Wake _____
Sleep _____ Wake _____
Sleep _____ Wake _____
Sleep _____ Wake _____

YOUR TIME
What was your greatest accomplishment today?

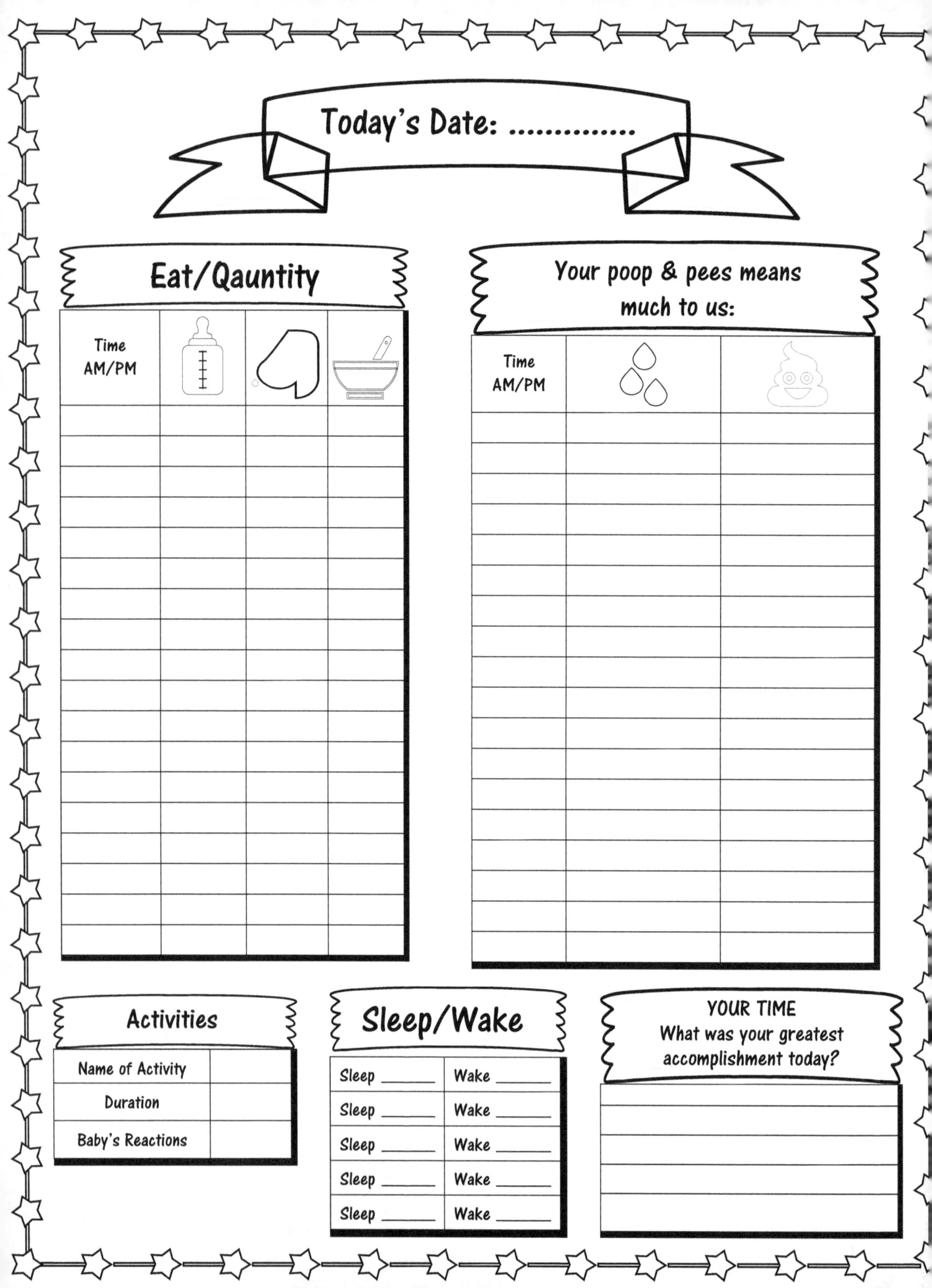

Today's Date: ....

Eat/Qauntity

Time AM/PM	🍼	🤱	🥣

Your poop & pees means much to us:

Time AM/PM	💧	💩

Activities

Name of Activity	
Duration	
Baby's Reactions	

Sleep/Wake

Sleep _____ Wake _____
Sleep _____ Wake _____
Sleep _____ Wake _____
Sleep _____ Wake _____
Sleep _____ Wake _____

YOUR TIME
What was your greatest accomplishment today?

Today's Date: ....

Eat/Qauntity

Time AM/PM	🍼	🤱	🥣

Your poop & pees means much to us:

Time AM/PM	💧	💩

Activities

Name of Activity	
Duration	
Baby's Reactions	

Sleep/Wake

Sleep _____ Wake _____
Sleep _____ Wake _____
Sleep _____ Wake _____
Sleep _____ Wake _____
Sleep _____ Wake _____

YOUR TIME
What was your greatest accomplishment today?

Today's Date: ....

Eat/Qauntity

Time AM/PM	🍼	🤱	🥣

Your poop & pees means much to us:

Time AM/PM	💧	💩

Activities

Name of Activity	
Duration	
Baby's Reactions	

Sleep/Wake

Sleep _____ Wake _____

Sleep _____ Wake _____

Sleep _____ Wake _____

Sleep _____ Wake _____

Sleep _____ Wake _____

YOUR TIME
What was your greatest accomplishment today?

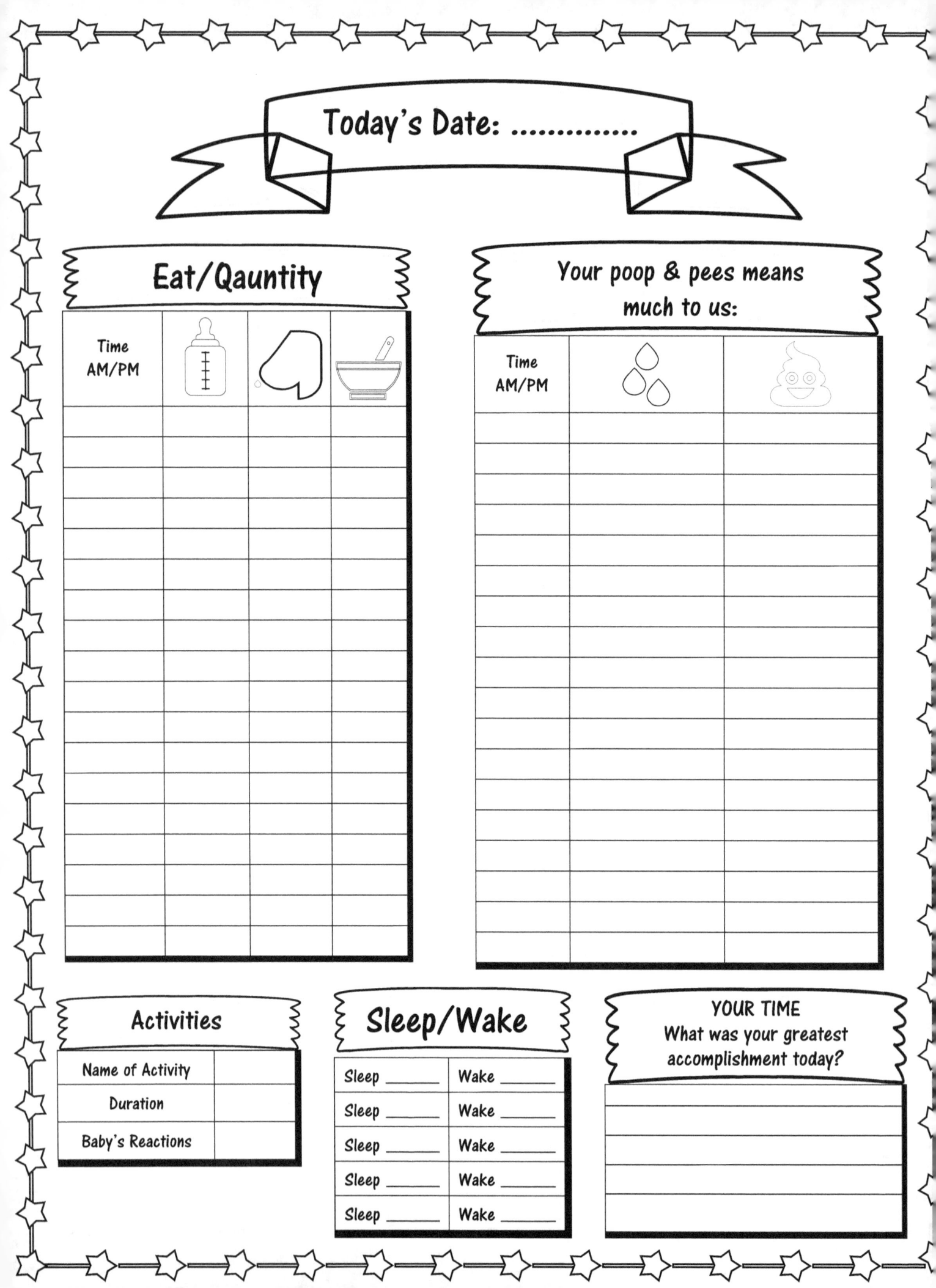

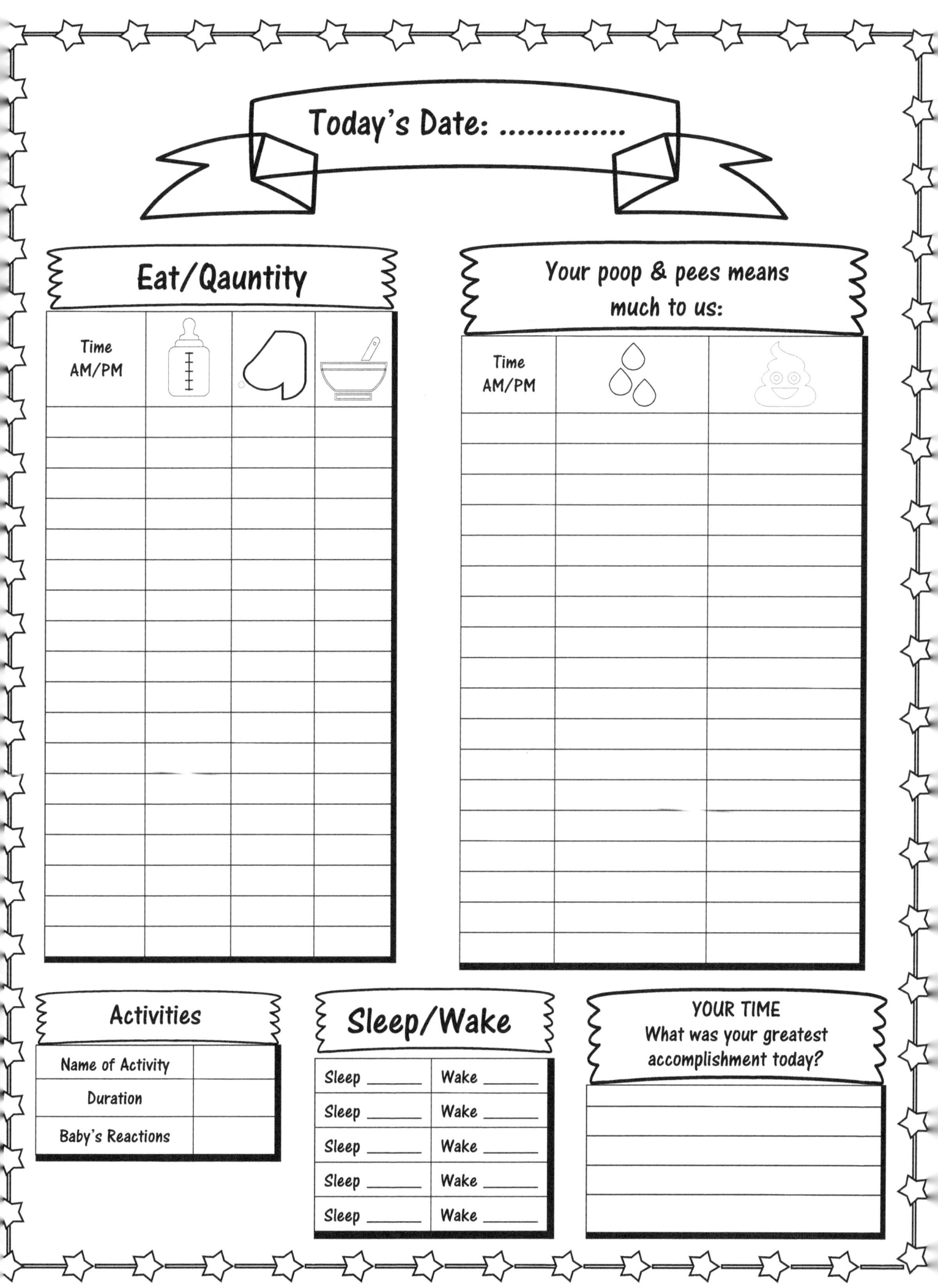

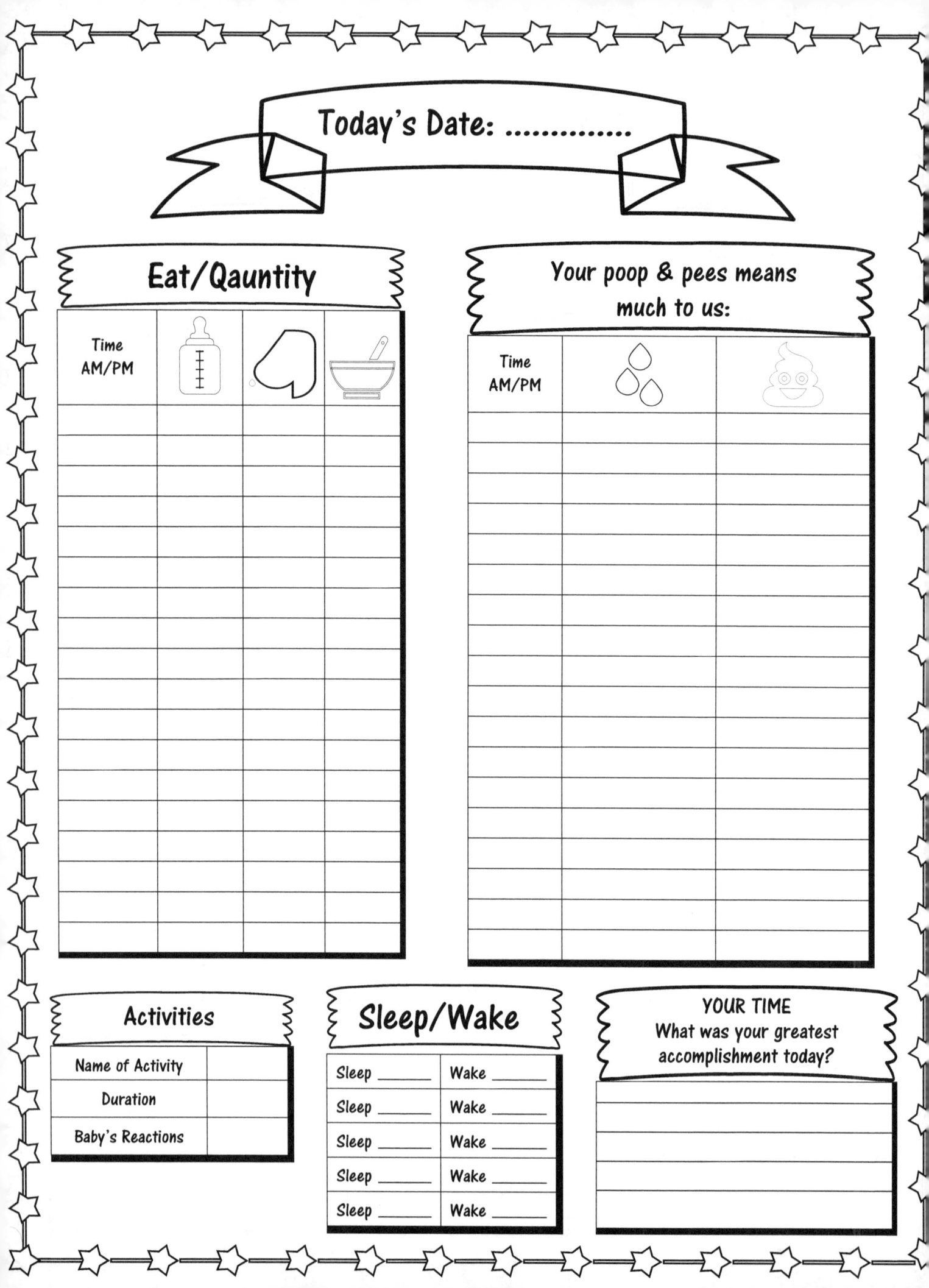

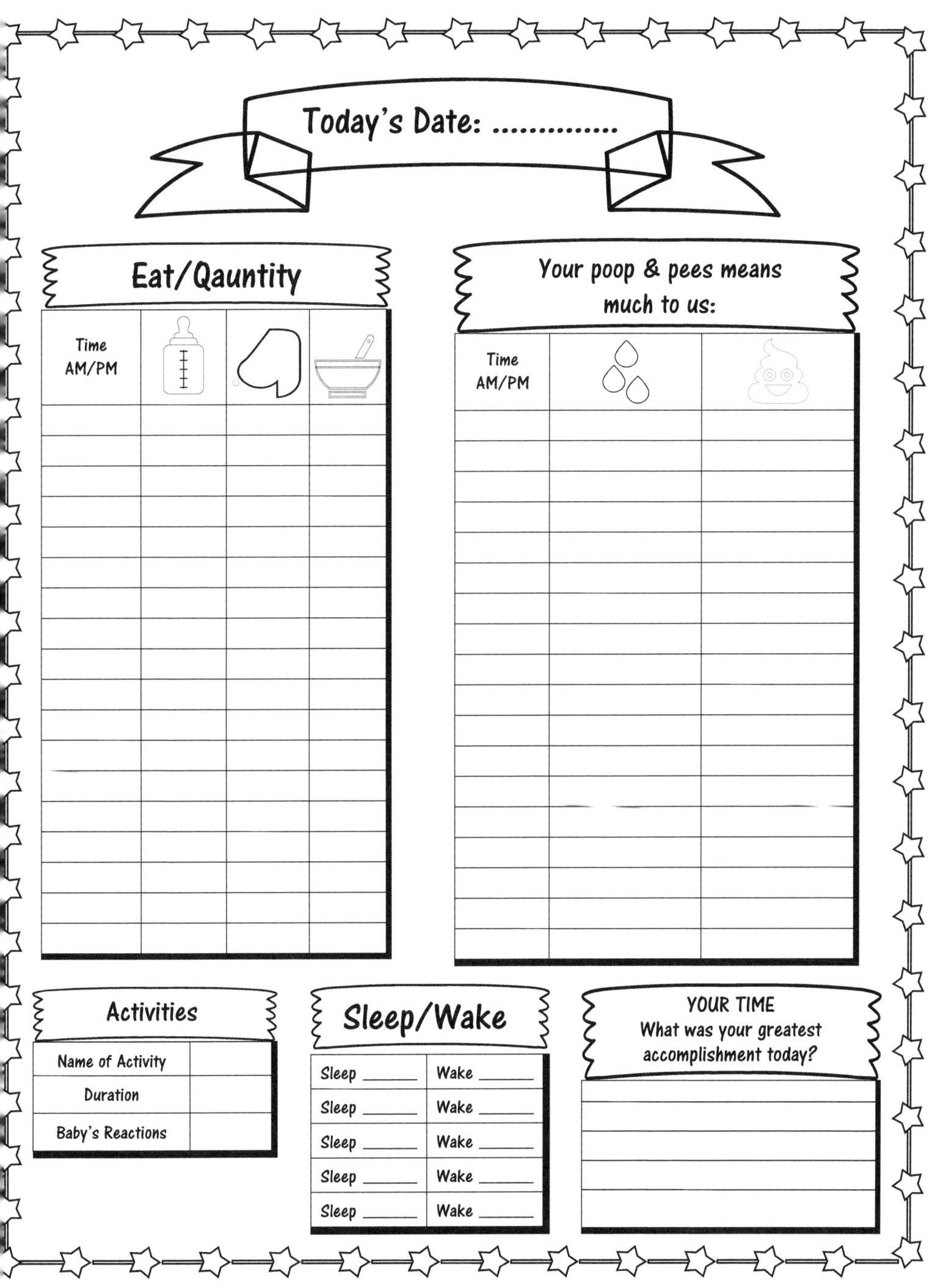

Today's Date: ....

Eat/Qauntity

Time AM/PM	🍼	🥛	🥣

Your poop & pees means much to us:

Time AM/PM	💧	💩

Activities

Name of Activity	
Duration	
Baby's Reactions	

Sleep/Wake

Sleep _____ Wake _____
Sleep _____ Wake _____
Sleep _____ Wake _____
Sleep _____ Wake _____
Sleep _____ Wake _____

YOUR TIME
What was your greatest accomplishment today?

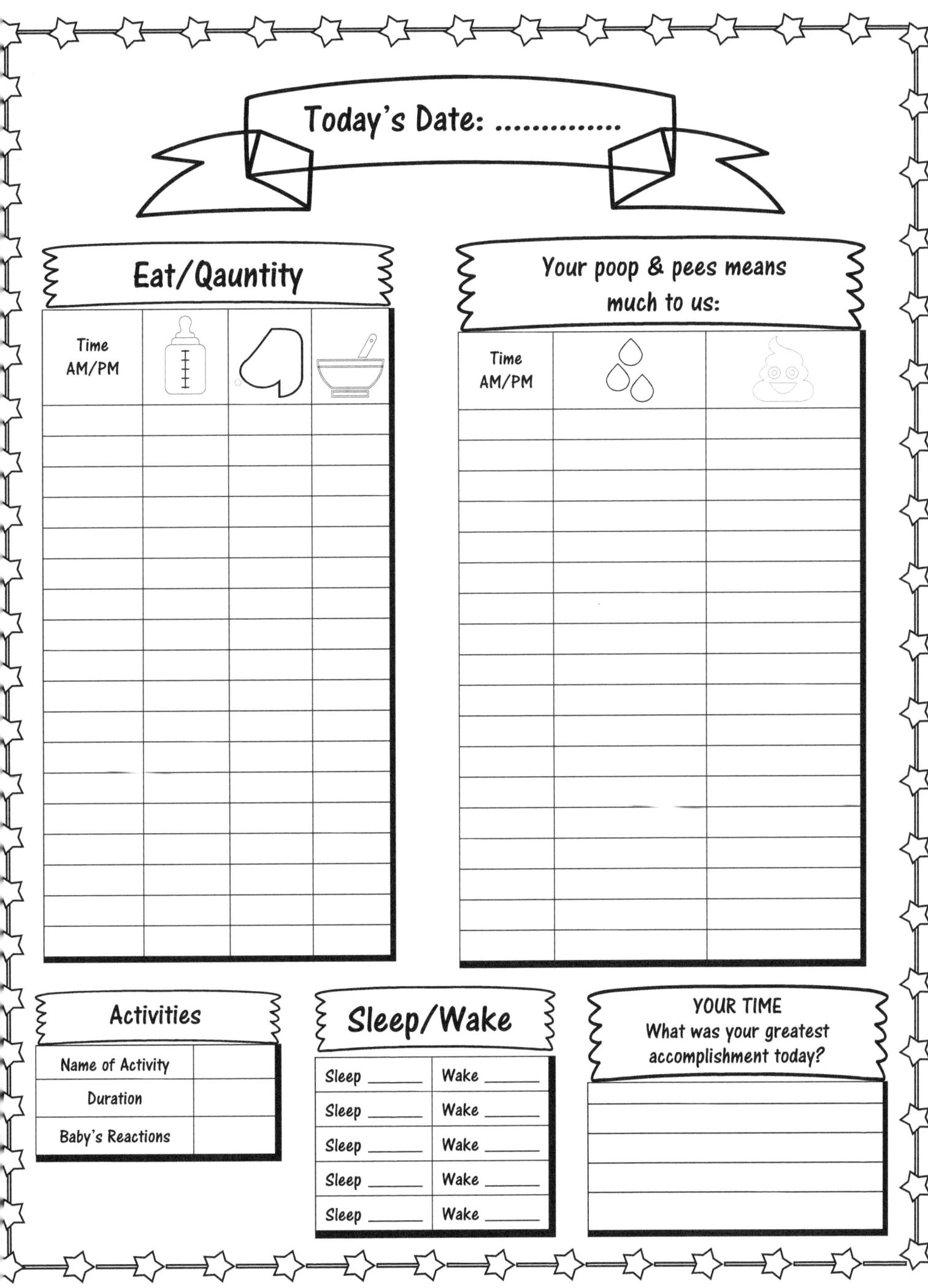

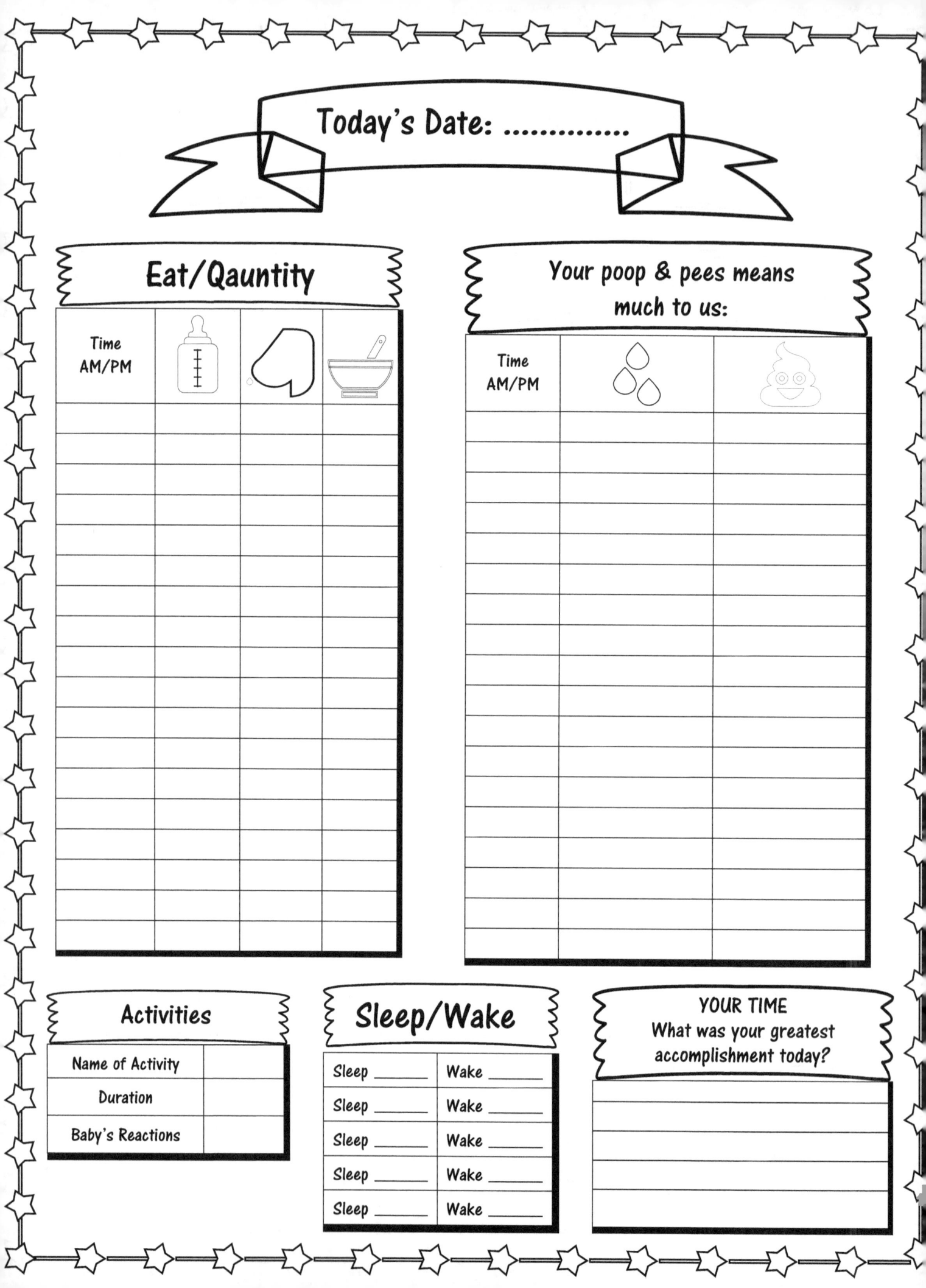

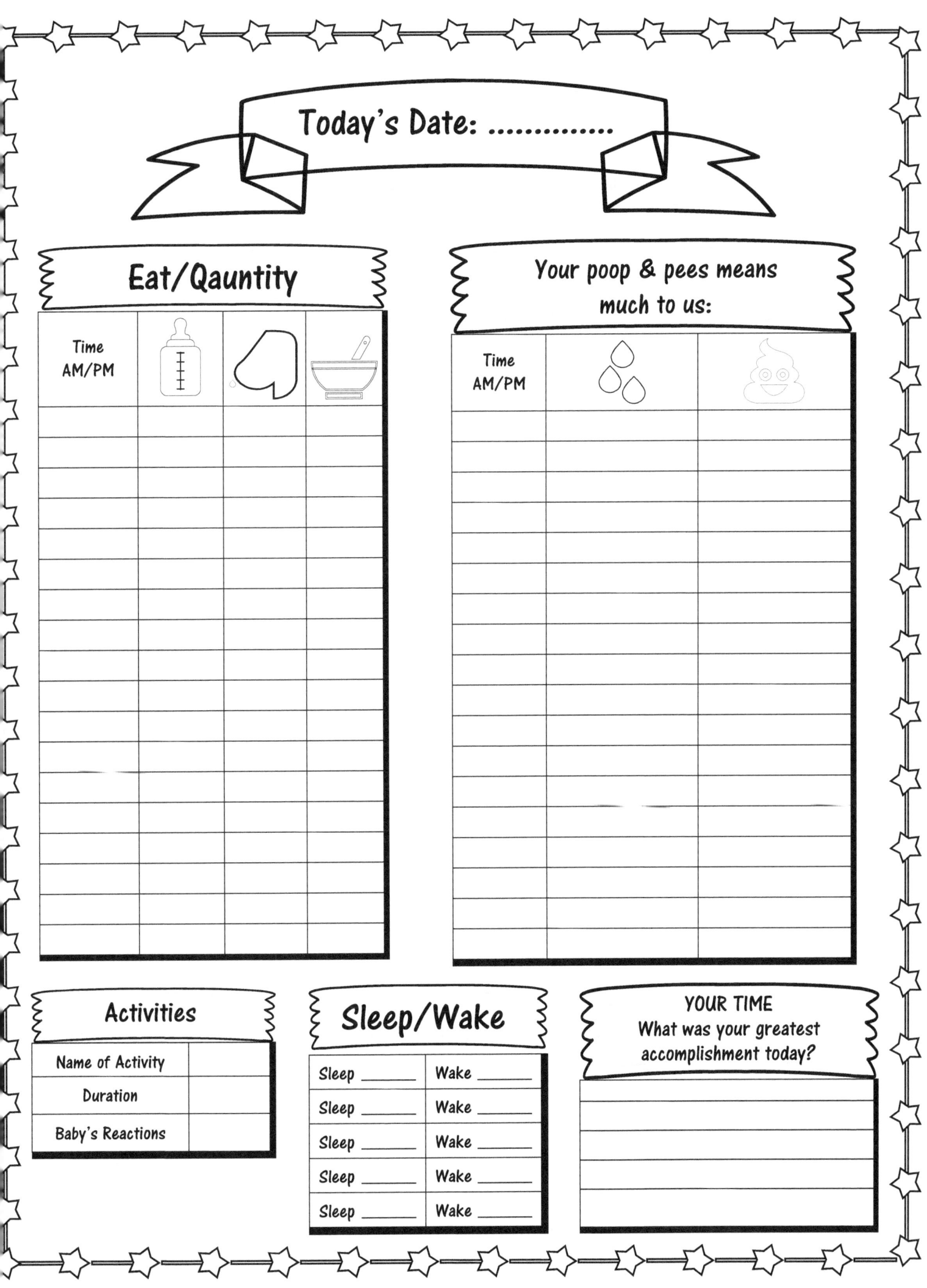

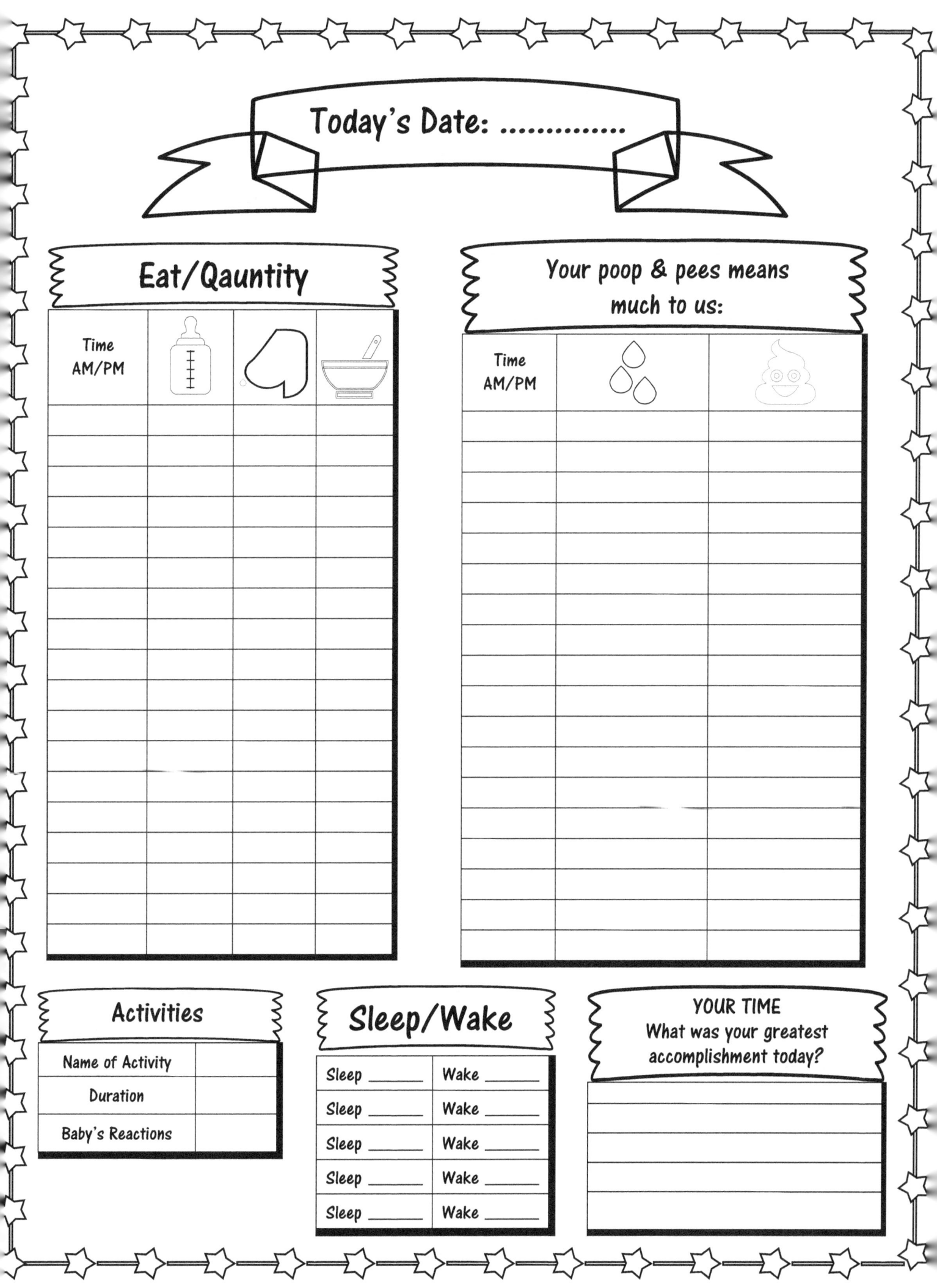

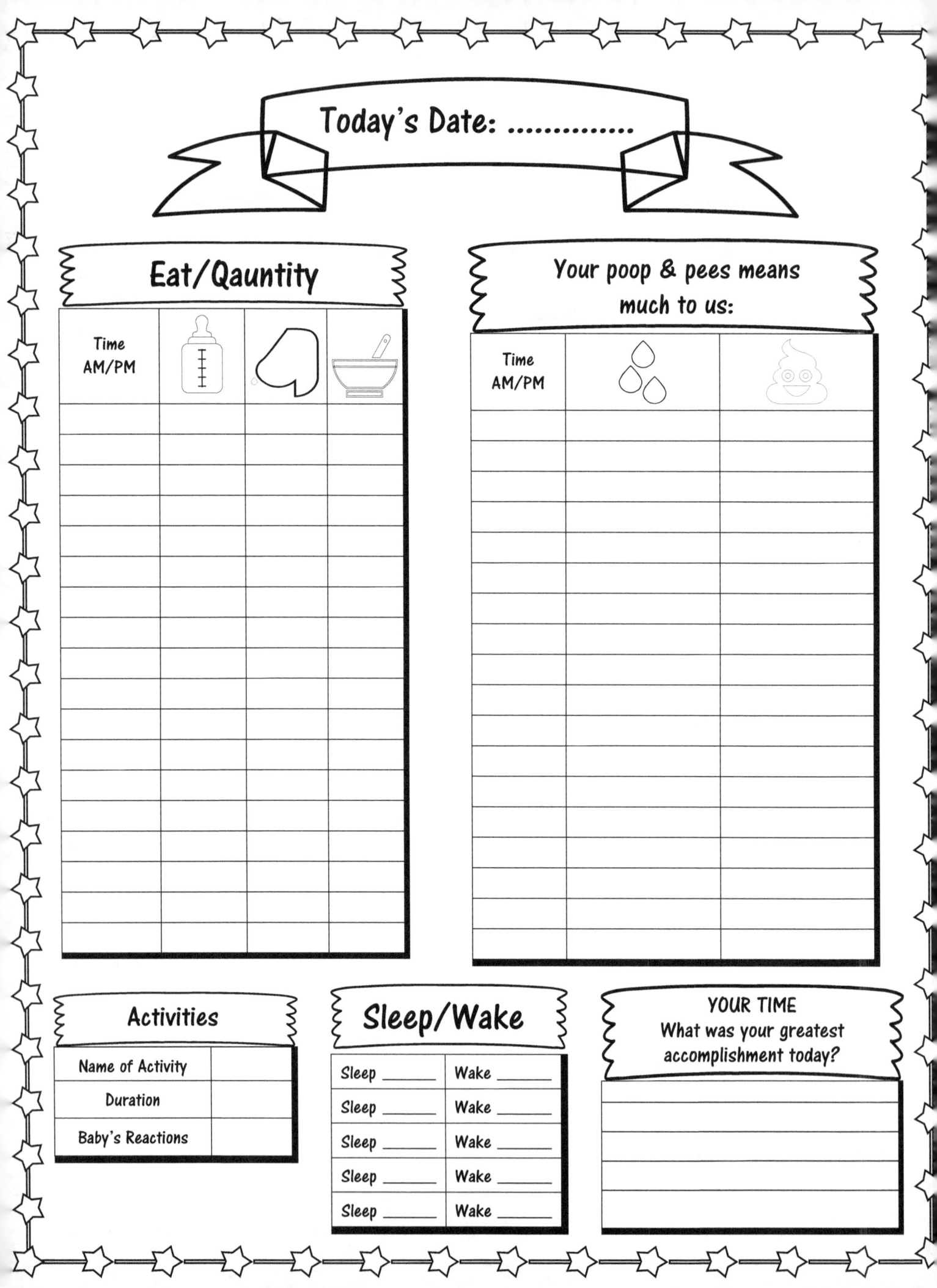

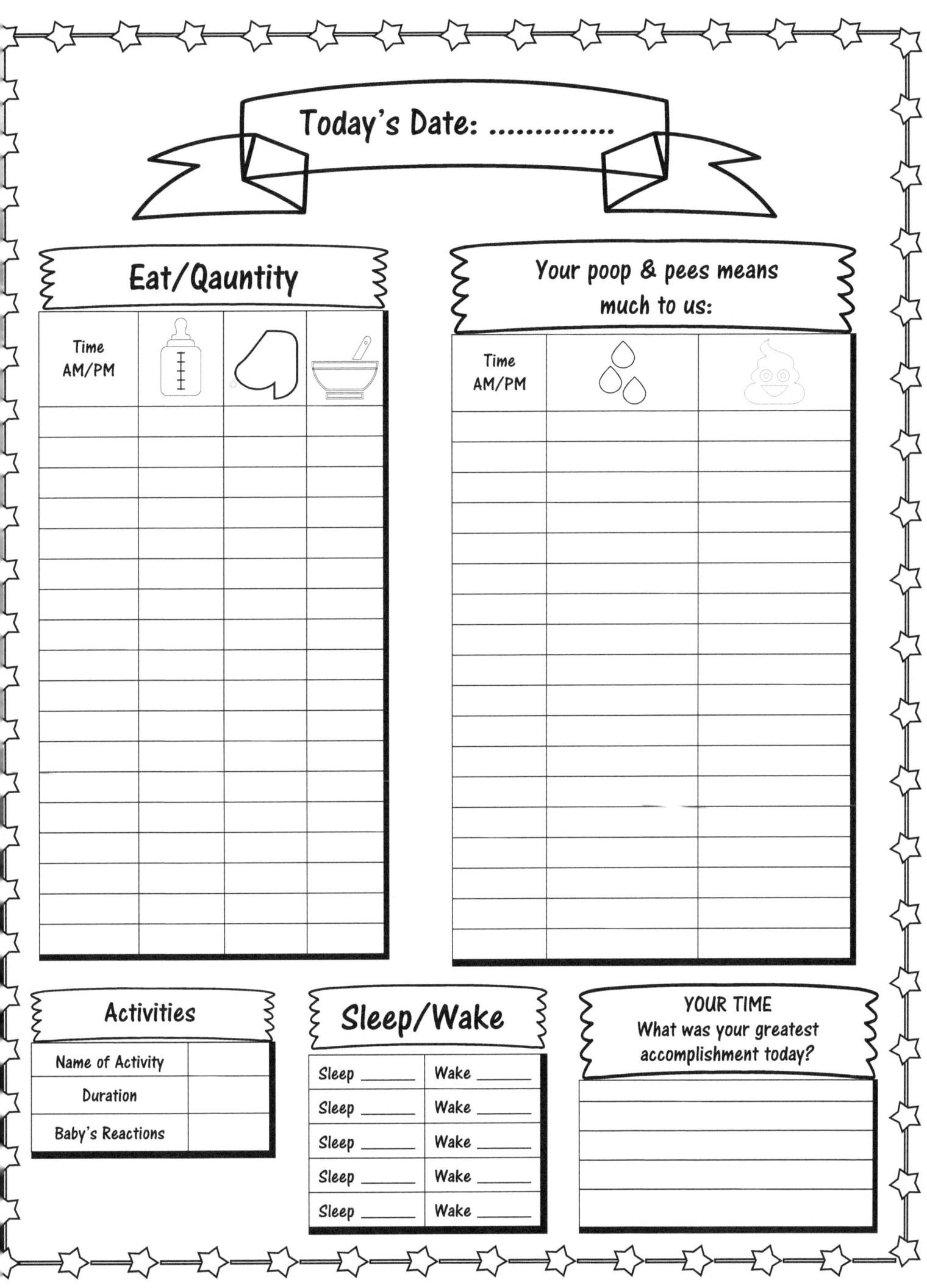

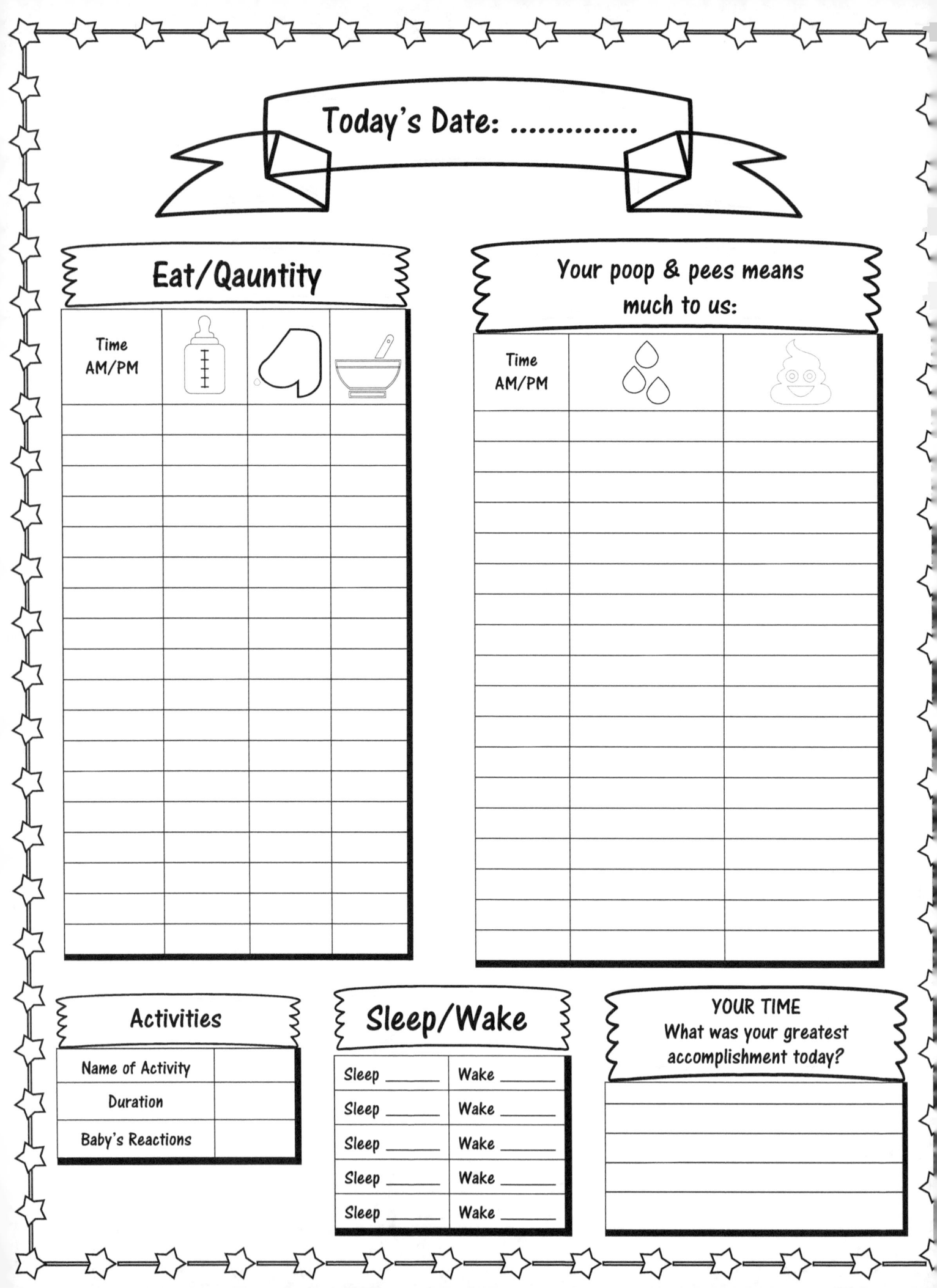

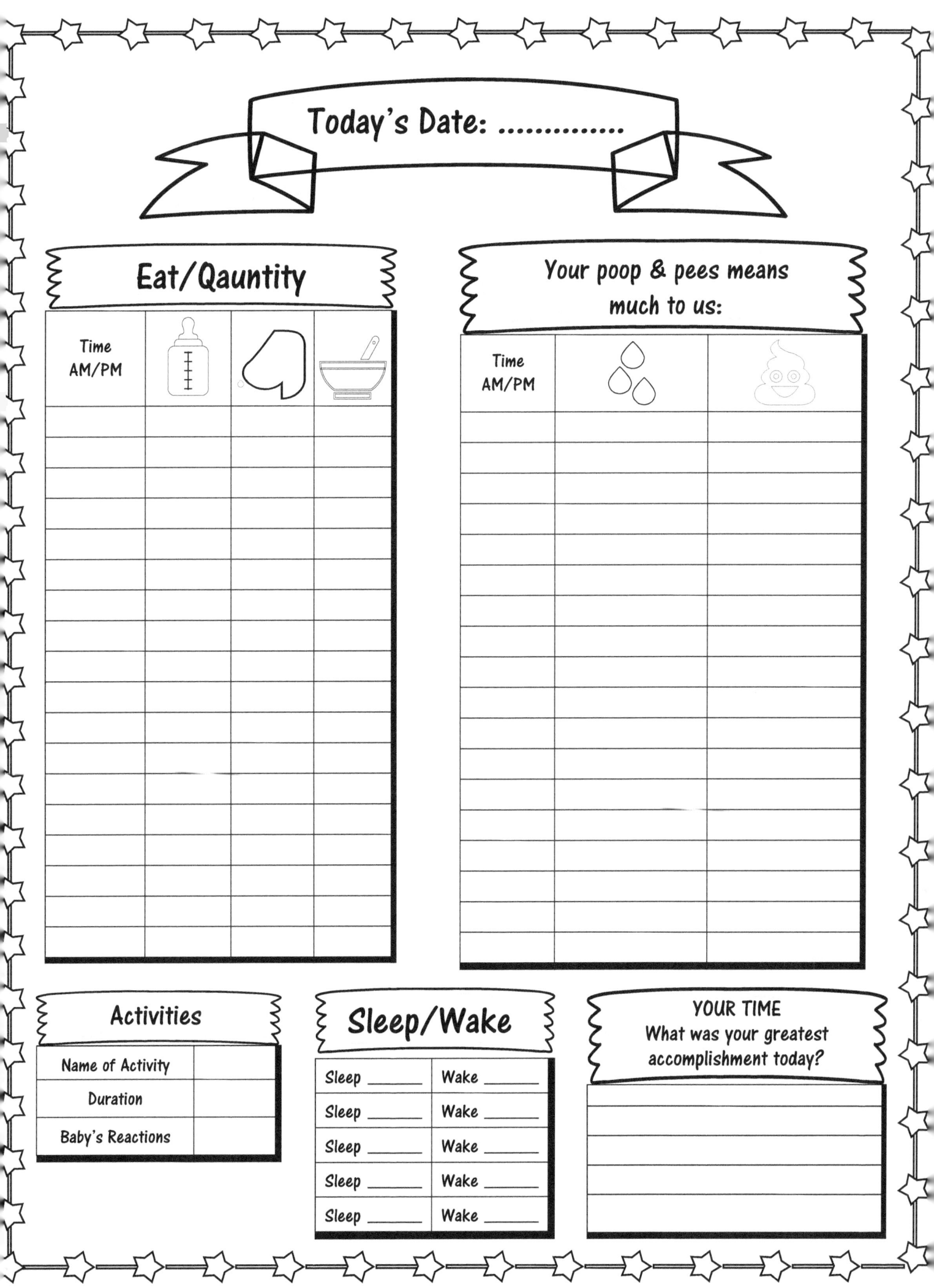

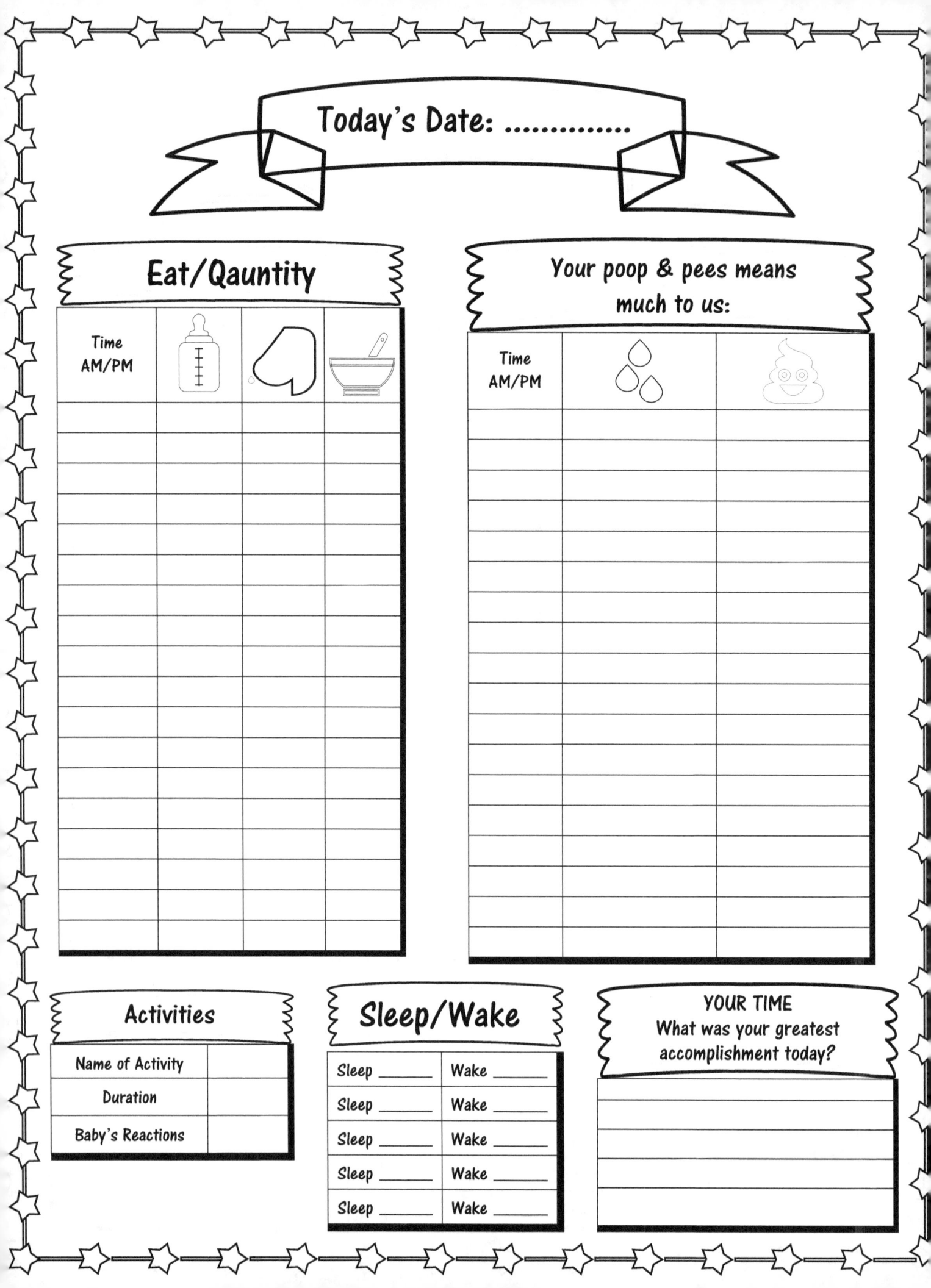

www.ingramcontent.com/pod-product-compliance
Lightning Source LLC
Chambersburg PA
CBHW081508080526
44589CB00017B/2696